WITHDRAWN

Contents

Introduction

For the first ten years of its existence the Intermediate Technology Development Group was exclusively concerned with the problems of Third World technology. In 1975 a generous grant from the Gatsby Charitable Foundation made it possible to start a project concerned with the application of the concepts of 'appropriate technology' to the British urban economy. This initiative expressed our belief that it is necessary to change the direction of all economies, no matter what the present state of their development may be in order that they will in time converge instead of diverging as they do at present. It is a practical recognition of the fact that rich and poor countries alike stand in need of a new kind of technology, one that is more in harmony with people, and with the living and inanimate environment of which we are all a part.

John Davis, who for the past three years has been responsible for what has become known as the AT-UK Unit of ITDG, has spoken on many aspects of 'AT for Britain' at numerous meetings and conferences. In addition to a twice yearly newsletter, he has written various papers and articles that have aroused considerable interest.

This booklet has been compiled from these writings by Roger England in order that a wider group of people at home and overseas may see in simple outline some of the most significant issues that have emerged in the course of this project — the search for more appropriate ways of meeting the material needs of people in a densely populated industrial society.

George McRobie, Chairman ITDG.

Technology For a Changing World

Compiled by Roger England
from a series of papers by
John Davis

Intermediate Technology Publications Ltd.

Published by Intermediate Technology Publications Ltd.,
9 King Street, London WC2 8HN

© Intermediate Technology Publications Ltd., 1978
ISBN: 0 903031 56 6

Typeset by Texet, Leighton Buzzard, Beds. and
Printed by The Russell Press Ltd., Nottingham

1

How Appropriate is Conventional Technology?

The next few decades will bring a number of quite fundamental changes to modern industrial countries. Over this period we shall be leaving behind much of the materialistic society with its ever-increasing consumption of goods and moving into a world of different values in which *quality of life* will be seen as being of greater importance than, and quite different from, *quantity of consumption*.

Our technologies — our ways of doing and making things — are intimately bound-up with this change. Increasingly, the problems caused by our prevailing technologies heighten our perception to the need for this change in social attitudes whilst, at the same time, dissatisfaction with many aspects of contemporary society are resulting in mounting pressure for changes in our technologies. This transition from the materialistic society will not be a simple one, nor one that is easily or painlessly achieved. As with all periods of significant and accelerated social transition, there will be great resistance from those gaining from the old order. Technologies are not neutral: they reflect prevailing interests and currently these interests are those of large companies and organised labour.

Whilst we shall mainly be concerned here with the problems of contemporary technologies and viable alternatives to them that are more suitable for the quality of life era, it would be foolish not to recognise that these contemporary technologies have achieved a great deal. Particularly in the post-war decades of intense reconstruction when the prevailing philosophy has been to apply as much advanced technology as possible in order to create economic growth, a considerable measure of success has been achieved in most industrial countries. Even in countries such as Britain where growth rates have been at very modest levels, a marked improvement in average living standards resulted, and substantial progress was made in providing public facilities and services. This could not have happened if it had not been

1

for the productivity increases achieved in industry and other parts of the economy through the introduction of new technologies. The magnitude of growth achieved in these industrialised countries was directly proportional to their investment in modern technologies and their effective use of those investments.

To point to the need for change in the 1980's is not to negate those achievements, nor to imply that there is nothing beneficial and desirable in the technologies that facilitated them; our densely populated island would be in a sorry state without them. All may not be well but certainly all is not wrong, though a new direction is required. As we move into the quality of life age we must seek technologies more appropriate to it. These appropriate technologies will not be based on a rejection of all that modern science and technology have provided: there is no question of turning back to primitive technologies. Technologies appropriate to the new age will require the very best that human skill and ingenuity can contrive but they will be conditioned by a different set of priorities under which many of the present unsatisfactory characteristics will be discarded.

Sources of Concern
In the early years of post-war development there was widespread feeling that the major problems of production and distribution had been solved — at least we knew where we were going. Serious and sustained criticisms were seldom heard as, with only occasional and relatively minor cyclical setbacks, national economies in Europe and North America expanded without serious inflation and with full employment. By the end of the sixties, however, concern began to be expressed, most notably about the environmental consequences of unlimited industrial expansion, the undesirable stress experienced by many workers, particularly those in the high volume production end of industry, and the problems of international resource depletion. Doubts were also expressed about the real ability of a growth economy to automatically solve the problems of the poorer social groups. Many of these concerns have since been brought sharply into focus and dramatically given more impetus by subsequent events, including the steep price rises in commodities and energy.

Although there are various and great differences between the production and distribution systems of all highly-developed countries, there are many important characteristics that they all share. From the point of view of technology, probably the most significant shared feature is the high volume, centralised mass production of an increasingly wide range of goods which has progressively replaced more localised and small-scale manufacture of almost all consumer products.

With historical hindsight it is possible to see that these systems of production and distribution were based on a series of assumptions

2

about our economic, social and political affairs and values. Some examples of these assumptions can be given by way of illustration:
— It is desirable that the labour and skill of people should be replaced by machines.
— Bigger is better in technology and in organisations.
— Growth in GNP is a good measure of economic progress; there is no limit to the riches that we all can enjoy and it is simply a matter of time before the poor become rich.
— Increasing capital investment is a sound foundation for industrial development.
— High volume production is the only route to low cost products and first cost (the cost of manufacturing) is the best measure of the true value of an article.
— Science-based technologies will solve the world's problem of production.
— The earth's resources can be treated as unlimited for all practical purposes.
— Monetary rewards will compensate for lack of job satisfaction.
— The capacity of the environment to withstand pollution is unlimited.

In the earlier stages of industrial development many, though by no means all, of these assumptions had some validity. For example, when production units were very small there was usually a marked advantage to be gained by expansion, and the replacement of much manual toil by the introduction of machinery was certainly a liberating development for large numbers of workers. But with the growth of the system many of these assumptions are now questionable, to say the least. It is because of the indiscriminate way in which the process of development has been pursued that some of the most undesirable distortions have occurred. The fallacies in many of these assumptions relate directly to what are currently being expressed as major causes of concern with our present-day technologies.

Whilst it is not the intention of this book to attempt an exhaustive analysis of these concerns, it is necessary to discuss them so that, in designing our appropriate technologies for the future, we can be clear about the type of situation we want to avoid. These will be discussed under two broad headings.

i) *Size, complexity and centralisation*
Many of the concerns expressed with our modern system of technologies can be related to the large-size, unnecessary complexity and degree of centralisation of production units and organisations. Not least among these is the alienation felt by many people from their work and, indeed, the whole productive process. Despite the undoubted material benefits that the growth economy has brought to the majority of working people and the welfare society that has been created from its surplus, there

3

are, however, widespread and growing feelings of injustice and helplessness arising from a sense of personal dependence on a system of inhuman scale and character, and of incomprehensible complexity. A situation has developed in which the material wealth of the nation is produced by a steadily decreasing proportion of the population in jobs which are often fragmented, de-skilled and unsatisfying. In earlier times it was often the case that tools and machines allowed people to make better use of their skills and abilities and thereby increased their sense of personal fulfilment. But once the imperatives of high volume mass production took control, tasks were fragmented to a point where they became meaningless, and workers became the slaves of their machines — or rather the machines of others. The resulting sense of alienation and dissatisfaction, particularly in the bigger factories and in industries where competitive pressures are greatest, has heightened the feeling of class difference and soured relationships between shop floor and management, and also between shop floor and trade union. The indiscriminate pursuit of bigness has also led to a poor mixture of employment opportunities in many districts because of the concentration on a few large units.

Damage to the environment — air pollution, noise, soil erosion, water and sea pollution, congestion and solid waste disposal — is to a considerable extent a function of concentrated industrialisation not only of manufacturing industries but also of many of the institutions of modern society. Its effects are pervasive and are accentuated both by the concentration of industry into larger units and by the related process of urbanisation. Industrial concentration and urbanisation are nowhere greater than in Britain. The facts of environmental pollution are becoming well documented and it is not our intention to go into detail here. We may speculate, however, that in addition to the harmful physical effects of pollution, the combination of such high degrees of urbanisation and industrial giantism is a factor contributing to widespread social dissatisfaction. The unnatural environment in which many people now live and work breeds an ignorance of the processes of nature and man's interdependence with the natural environment upon which survival depends. The effects of giantism are not confined to industry and can also be seen in agriculture where an exploitative industrial approach drains the land of its natural properties which must then be substituted by expensive, imported and high energy-dependent chemicals. Urbanisation and giantism have gone too far, with damaging environmental consequences.

Even in narrow terms of productivity, the problem of determining the most appropriate scale of plant and organisation for any particular industry is not one with a simple or unique solution. Certainly bigger is not always better and in fact there can be no sweeping generalisation made about this aspect of industry as a whole. The worst errors are made when the focus of attention is on machine or plant theoretical productivity, and the wide range of other relevant factors such as marketing, management, competition, distribution, labour relations, market fluctuations, supply constraints etc. are ignored or given inadequate consideration. Too often, probably because they are more easily quantifiable, the theoretical economies of scale of technology are given undue importance. The pressure to squeeze out marginal improvements in factory gate unit costs push the scale of operation ever higher despite many practical considerations that would favour a smaller operation, and there is a growing conviction that some industries have gone much too far. For many finished product manufacturing industries, the maximum adverse effect on factory gate unit costs that would be caused by a reduction in plant size to around one-third of the theoretical optimum, is seldom more than 5% and is more often 2-3%. Such small differences can very easily be outweighed by other cost factor differences both inside and outside the factory.

In bread-making the search for bigness and economies of scale led to a situation whereby three major companies were responsible for almost three-quarters of all bread production. At the turn of this century a 2lb loaf of home-baked bread cost about one old penny (about ½p). Allowing for a 20-fold fall in the value of money this would amount to about 10p in present values. But the shop price of a comparable loaf made by one of the major producers is now about 25p whereas the cost of a home baked loaf is about 15p. It does not appear, therefore, that the process of industrialisation either of bread-making or flour milling has contributed to a reduction in the real cost (not to mention quality) of this basic foodstuff: on the contrary, it would appear to have increased the cost substantially. Baking a loaf in the kitchen, we are now paying about 1.5 times the cost paid at the beginning of the century, and a factory loaf costs 2.5 times as much. The reason for the more costly loaf is no doubt related to some extent to the levy of substantial revenue (more than 30% of all added value) on all commercial activities as well as to there being no labour charge for a home-produced product. It is not surprising then that the trend to large factory baking has been reversed and an increasing proportion of bread is now being produced in High Street bakeries and domestic kitchens despite the high prices charged to small bakers and householders for flour.

In a similar way, the brewing industry has been almost completely industrialised in the past fifty years and hundreds of small local breweries have been replaced by giant factories owned by about six major companies. Their domination of the business has been greatly enhanced by their control of the important tied-house section of the market, but otherwise their development has closely followed the pattern of the baking industry through takeover and closure of local firms thus reducing competition. Comparison of the cost of the products of the modern brewing industry with those of traditional local breweries which prevailed previously is complicated by the high duties currently raised from the sale of beer. When due allowance is made for this, however, it does not appear that industrialisation of the brewing industry has resulted in any cheaper product despite the huge investment in factories, depots and fleets of delivery vehicles. Indeed, the recent emergence of a successful small brewery at Blackawton in Devon—operated entirely as a one man business and supplying 25 neighbouring free houses with 1,500 gallons per week — confirms that any economies of scale that may exist in processing beer are at least offset by the high overheads and distribution costs of a big company operation. Very recently a small new independent brewery has been started in London — the first for 100 years.

In the light of experience it would seem that various other industries, including garment manufacturing, food processing, paper manufacturing and some sections of the engineering industry, are already reviewing their policies on plant size. But although a move towards more and smaller production units within existing companies is likely to produce some worthwhile improvements, not least of which may be improved labour relations, it will not basically change production and distribution systems that have grown very complex, costly and inefficient. If we are to develop technologies more appropriate to the new age it is unlikely that they will come from a scaling down of existing operations. They are much more likely to be achieved by a fresh approach from small new-growth points.

ii) *Resources, energy and waste*
Other concerns expressed about our modern technologies (which suggest that many of them are unsuitable for the future) are focussed on the way in which they utilise resources and energy. Implicit in the factory-based mass production system for industry (and agriculture) is the assumption that raw material supplies and fuels are both cheap and plentiful and that the more men that can be replaced by machines the better. As a consequence, we in Britain import millions of tons of raw materials (two-thirds of our total consumption) at enormous cost to convert them into goods nearly all of which are thrown on the scrap heap within about 10 years. The adoption of high volume production methods combined with product designs of decreasing durability has been made acceptable to the consumer through an emphasis on minimum first cost for products, and through product design fashions promoted through advertising. As a result, consumer attitudes have substantially changed with much less importance now being attached to the whole-life cost of an article. There can be little doubt that this was a choice made by manufacturers of durable goods — often slavishly following American precedents — with the acquiescence of both consumers and employees. Furthermore, it was this development that has created the worst type of industrial employment — the mass production line

assembly system with all the undesirable personal and social consequences mentioned earlier.

The high volume production system is dependent upon mistaken beliefs that first cost minimisation is a desirable objective and that in a world of unlimited material and energy resources it is acceptable to produce short-life, throw-away articles. The real practical consequence of this is that an enormous, ever-increasing proportion of resources and energy is devoted to the production of waste (and pollution). Of course, material and energy resources are far from unlimited. In order to conserve them we must replace the objective of first cost minimisation with that of minimising the life cost of products. The vital importance of this is emphasised by the fact that roughly three-quarters of all industrial energy consumption is associated with the production of basic materials like steel, cement and so on, whilst only about one-quarter is used in the transformation of materials into finished goods. Consequently, maximum saving of energy is achieved when finished articles are repaired and reconditioned rather than replaced by new ones involving the production of more basic materials. A switch of emphasis to minimum life cost products would achieve quite dramatic savings in energy and materials. It has, of course, been alleged that such a basic change of technology would be entirely unacceptable because of the effect on employment. In order to evaluate this effect, the Social Affairs Division of the EEC have sponsored a research project undertaken by the Battelle Institute in Geneva. This study shows that in the car industry, whereas factory employment would be virtually halved if average car life was increased from 10 to 20 years, jobs created in the maintenance, repair and reconditioning business would more than compensate for loss of this factory employment. Thus about half the work force would benefit from the more humane conditions prevailing in the servicing sector since reconditioning work is a more skilled and satisfying employment, best carried out in comparatively small workshops scattered widely throughout the country. Some alleviation of the problems of concentration and centralisation would also be achieved. The adoption of a more durable product philosophy with emphasis on whole-life costs rather than on first cost would also provide a unique opportunity to create more satisfying employment in the manufacturing process itself. It seems likely that in the car industry at least a doubling of product life could probably be obtained at a cost increase of about 20%. Bearing in mind the very large material and energy savings to be made when two short-life cars are replaced by one, there is considerable scope for spending more money on labour input during manufacture without increasing the cost of motoring per annum.

Technology for the Transition
We have looked briefly at some of the concerns and problems of our contemporary technologies. It is quite clear that, regardless of how

7

much worse many of these concerns may become in the future, our present technologies and the institutional forms in which they are practised are far from ideal or optimal. Even if we were not at an important crossroads in our technological development, any reasonable evaluation of our technological performance which encompassed dimensions of efficiency, social desirability, environment, energy, resource consumption rates and so on could only conclude that many of our present technologies are indeed third rate. The same must be said for the kind of thinking that wishes only to increase the scale of these technologies. We must search for new and superior forms of technology based on sound design and problem-solving i.e. for a first rate technology that is appropriate in all its dimensions. The proposals for changes of emphasis in the production and distribution systems and their associated technologies which follow are based on the assumption that there is a consensus wish to maintain and, where possible, improve upon the present material standards of the population and at the same time to provide sufficient resources to enhance the general quality of life within a mixed economy and compassionate society. We are not concerned here with the problems of a society which has already reached a limit of its development. Neither are we concerned with the pursuit of an increasing Gross Domestic Product for its own sake but rather with a change in the direction of development.

In this difficult period of transition we shall need to create a greater sense of community than has existed for many years. People will need to feel that they are working for the common good and to achieve this they will need to have returned to them a sense of self-reliance. Their actions and efforts must have a more immediate effect in their own work and living environments, and the present widespread sense of helplessness and dependence must disappear.

It would be a pretence to maintain that the answers to these problems are readily available but it is the thesis of this book that our technologies will play a central role. In the light of what we can now see as problems with our present system, it is maintained that the required transitional change in direction can best be achieved in three ways:

— The regeneration of small-scale, geographically dispersed manufacturing units (particularly in those industries where the economies of scale are not great) in ways which will encourage individual commitment to their success, and which complement operations which must necessarily continue on a large-scale, centralised basis.

— Elimination of the prodigious amount of unnecessary waste that exists throughout our present systems whilst at the same time ensuring that the maximum benefit from these savings goes to the neediest sections of the community.

— The reduction of our national dependence on imports by a more intensive development of our own human, land and raw material resources.

8

To neglect any of these three objectives and to persist on our present course of wasteful, dependent development moving towards an increasingly centralised and monolithic industrial mix will not only place intolerable pressure on the whole population but will be most damaging to the poorest section of the community, and to the maintenance of a compassionate society. A further and no less important consequence would be an amplification of international tensions particularly between ourselves and the Third World nations.

It is important to note that the above-mentioned three changes in direction are mutually reinforcing in many respects. It is obvious also that economy in energy and material utilisation can make substantial contributions towards a reduction of environmental pollution, particularly if it is accompanied by a certain amount of geographical disperson of manufacturing activities. Simultaneously, small-scale and geographically dispersed manufacturing provides the possibility of a wider variety of satisfying employment on a local basis.

Perhaps the most important potential benefit of all will be the change in personal and community attitude that could accompany this new emphasis. There can be no true compassion in a society that does not really care what it produces, how it is made, nor what happens when it no longer serves a useful purpose. Indifference to the natural world and to the community easily becomes a consequence of carelessness about material things and vice versa. In 1928, Bernard Shaw wrote the following in his book "The Intelligent Woman's Guide to Socialism, Capitalism, Sovietism and Facism" in the section headed How Wealth Accumulates and Men Decay:

"I want to stress this personal helplessness we are all stricken with in the face of a system that has passed beyond our knowledge and control. To bring it nearer home, I propose that we switch off from big things like empires and their wars to little familiar things. Take pins for example! I do not know why it is that I so seldom use a pin when my wife cannot get on without boxes of them at hand; but it is so: and I will therefore take pins as being for some reason specially important to women.

There was a time when pinmakers could buy the material; shape it; make the head and the point; ornament it; and take it to market or to your door and sell it to you. They had to know three trades: buying, making, and selling; and the making required skill in several operations. They not only knew how the thing was done from beginning to end, but could do it. But they could not afford to sell you a paper of pins for a farthing. Pins cost so much that a woman's dress allowance was called pin money.

By the end of the eighteenth century Adam Smith boasted that it took eighteen men to make a pin, each man doing a little bit of the job and passing the pin on to the next, and none of them being able to make a whole pin or to buy the materials or to sell it when it was made. The most you could say for them was that at least they had some idea of how it was made, though they could not make it. Now as this meant that they were clearly less capable and knowledgeable men than the old pin-makers, you may ask why Adam Smith boasted of it as a triumph of civilization when its effect was so clearly a degrading effect. The reason was that by setting each man to do just one little bit of work and nothing but that, over and over again, he became very quick at it. The men, it is said, could turn out nearly five thousand pins a day each; and thus pins became plentiful and cheap. The country was supposed to be richer because it had more pins, though it had turned capable men into mere machines doing their work without intelligence, and being fed by the spare food of the capitalist as an engine is fed with coals and oil. That was why the poet Goldsmith, who was a far-sighted economist as well as a poet, complained that 'wealth accumulates, and men decay'.

Nowadays Adam Smith's eighteen men are as extinct as the dip-lodocus. The eighteen flesh-and-blood machines are replaced by machines of steel which spout out pins by the hundred million. Even sticking them into pink papers is done by machinery. The result is that with the exception of a few people who design the machines, nobody knows how to make a pin or how a pin is made: that is to say, the modern worker in pin manufacture need not be one-tenth so intelligent and skilful and accomplished as the old pinmaker; and the only compen-sation we have for this deterioration is that pins are so cheap that a single pin has no expressible value at all. Even with a big profit added to the cost price you can buy dozens for a farthing; and pins are so recklessly thrown away and wasted that verses have to be written to persuade children (without success) that it is a sin to steal a pin.

Many serious thinkers, like John Ruskin and William Morris, have been greatly troubled by this, just as Goldsmith was, and have asked whether we really believe that it is an advance in wealth to lose our skill and degrade our workers for the sake of being able to waste pins by the ton. We shall see later on when we come to consider the Dis-tribution of Leisure, that the cure for this is not to go back to the old ways; for if the saving of time by modern machinery was equally divided among us, it would set us all free for higher work than pin-making or the like. In the meantime, the fact remains that pins are now made by men and women who cannot make anything by themselves, and cannot even arrange between themselves to make anything, even part by part. They are ignorant and helpless, and cannot lift their finger to begin their day's work until it has all been arranged for them by their employers, who themselves do not understand the workings of the machines they buy, and simply pay other people to operate them according to the machine maker's directions.

The same is true of clothes. Formerly, the whole task of making clothes, from the shearing of the sheep to the turning out of the finished and washed garment ready to wear had to be done in the country by the men and women of the household (especially the women); to this day an unmarried woman is called a spinster. Nowadays, nothing is left of this but the sheep-shearing and even that, like the milking of cows, is being done by machinery. "

Shaw went onto say that if you give a woman a sheep today and ask her to produce a woollen dress and she will most likely be unable to do it. When she buys her clothes at a shop, she knows that there is a difference between wool and cotton and silk, between flannel and merino, and particularly between the artificial fibres, but as to how they are made and exactly what they are made of, she knows hardly anything, and the shop assistant is probably no wiser.

The capitalist system has produced an almost universal ignorance of the steps involved in manufacturing goods, whilst at the same time it encourages them to be produced on a gigantic scale. We have to buy books and encyclopaedias to find out the various processes in manufacturing, but as the books are often written by people who themselves are not experts, and who get their information from other books, what they tell is often out of date!

In our search for 'appropriate technologies' for the rest of the twentieth century it is clear that 'appropriate' must be understood to cover a wide range of dimensions. Of course, manufacturing units must survive economically and their technologies must be appropriate to enable them to do so. But appropriate also has a number of social and environmental dimensions such that, regardless of its technical efficiency, a technology can no longer be considered as appropriate if its social or environmental costs are too high. But we are looking for better than that. We are looking for a system of production and distribution that is not only acceptable, but that itself adds something to the quality of life by creating more worthwhile and satisfying work. Concepts of efficiency and appropriateness now mean much more than they did before.We must realise moreover, that the choice may not simply be between the 'appropriate technology' utopia and muddling along with our present system. Things could get much worse. In Britain at the moment the combination of a high level of consumption and social services, high dependence on foreign raw materials and food, poor industrial performance, high inflation, high unemployment and poor motivation make us highly vulnerable in a world of exploding population and commodity prices. Under these circumstances a continuation of our past high consumption, highly wasteful, throw-away system would seem to guarantee a future of real impoverishment and conflict which could be most damaging to the poorer sections of the community (including the elderly and infirm) and to the welfare society. It cannot make sense for a nation which is high in manpower but short of food and material resources to continue with a system that is prodigiously wasteful of all three.

11

Adoption of the broad objectives expressed earlier — growth in small-scale, decentralised manufacturing, elimination of energy wastage and reduction of dependence on imports — can help us overcome these problems. Their embodiment into future technology should contribute substantially to a healthy renewal/of Britain's material and cultural welfare — our future quality of life. Specifically, they will help to:
- create a high proportion of the productive new jobs required to provide worthwhile employment for about 1 million from unemployment, 1 million from private and public industry overmanning and 1 million from over-manned bureaucracies;
- move towards a greater degree of regional self-sufficiency in basic manufactures (to the extent socially desirable and economically feasible);
- create a better trade balance in manufactured goods by a reduction in national dependence on imported manufactures;
- increase the utilisation of indigenous resources;
- improve industrial flexibility, responsiveness to change, standards of delivery and product quality and reliability;
- provide a better small-scale industry complement to industry mix;
- provide work in small units which can be made more satisfying and personally fulfilling through the redesign of technologies and production organisation;
- greatly increase the use of waste energy and materials and used products of all kinds through recycling, processing and product renovation;
- reduce wasteful transportation in the distribution of goods and promote the most effective modes of transport;
- improve environmental conditions;
- provide opportunities for a substantial proportion of working people to participate in the ownership of their firm;
- alleviate some of the problems of industrial relations by reducing the size and complexity of many of our over-centralised and over-concentrated production units;
- recreate a sense of significance, pride and independence amongst a large section of the population.

A Taste of Appropriate Technology
The totality of technologies in an industrial society like Britain is immense and cannot be adequately dealt with here. Whilst we can broadly identify many of the types of change needed in our technologies we must recognise that it is as yet early days in the development of more appropriate technologies and no exhaustive list of superior technological alternatives exists. But there are examples and it is possible to identify some of the areas in which advances may be expected. These include:—

Low energy technologies
These are particularly vital to Britain given our unusual and insupportable level of energy consumption discussed elsewhere in this paper. Areas for new technologies include insulation systems, total-energy systems, energy storage systems, district heating systems, waste material processing (pyrolysis, incineration etc.) and heat pumps.

Alternative energy source technologies
Experience of the use in our climate of various forms of renewable sources of energy is now being accumulated. In addition to the now familiar solar panels for water heating, experimental buildings using the Trombe solar wall system have been constructed in the Wirral. Bungalows in Northern France have halved their space heating requirements with this method. As the capital cost of nuclear generating capacity increases from £500 per kilowatt installed towards £1,000, the prospects for tidal, wind and wave alternatives look increasingly attractive. Some of the new wind machine designs would appear to be competitive with thermal (fossil) power generation. Areas for new technologies include wind, wave, tidal, geothermal, hydrosystems, solar walls, cells, panels and organic systems.

Long-life product technologies
Over the past three decades consumer durables like furniture, electrical and other household goods etc. have suffered a much-reduced life expectancy. Most makes of car, at all price levels, last for only about ten years with the result that a car owner now consumes about five cars in a motoring lifetime. As a consequence the capital cost and the annual running cost now exceed those for a family house. The prospects for a long-life car (30 years or more) look good. Although first costs would be higher, real costs per annum could be considerably reduced. Furthermore, a change to more durable products would open up possibilities for more congenial and relatively small-scale manufacturing operations.

Second-life product technologies
These are products manufactured mainly from reconditioned, used components of scrap machines that are finished, presented and guaranteed under the same terms as similar products made from raw materials. There is now a steadily growing list of such products, either reconditioned whole machines such as IBM typewriters or photocopiers, or new machines built from used components of scrap machines such as earth moving equipment, food processing equipment, textile machinery, tractors, paper making machines etc.

Waste materials, separation and reprocessing technologies
Although dumping has been our favourite method of waste disposal there are the beginnings of new waste material reclamation and

reprocessing industries such as the Batchelor Robinson waste can reprocessing plant, North West Fibres kraft paper repulping in Liverpool, the National Freight Corporation sandwich building board made from waste plastics at Widnes etc. Areas for new technologies include fertilizer manufacture from sewage, animal feed processing from waste, plastics, paper, textile, board and metal reprocessing and industrial waste (fines) processing.

Small-scale food and drink technologies
After many years of concentration and centralisation in baking and brewing a reversal is beginning to take place with the emergence of high street hot bread shops and the renewed popularity of real beer from small local breweries. The economies of scale have turned out to be diseconomies after all. Other areas for new technologies include small-scale canneries.

Craft and semi-craft manufacture
Regeneration is occurring in many areas, particularly in small-scale clothing manufacture where the immensely costly distribution and inflexibility is overwhelming many of the mass production firms. As industrial factories close, the sales girls in a Great Missenden dress shop help make stock when they are not selling garments made by local women in their own homes. Other areas for small-scale manufacture include furniture and leather goods.

Natural materials processing
Whilst it would be foolish to pretend that synthetic materials have had their day, there are definite signs of a revival in natural fabrics. In the past few years, timber frame houses have again grown in popularity and there is a renewed interest in the use of stone in buildings. After a serious setback in the past decade, there is renewed hope for bricks through a marriage of ancient mud brick technology with glass-fibre reinforced cement rendering — a system originally developed for the Third World by John Parry but now being field tested by the Devon County Architect.

Transport and communications
Including motor/sailer cargo vessels, electric delivery vehicles and buses, and electronic communication systems.

Miniaturisation
Including electronic systems, microprocessors etc.

Subsequent sections of this book hope to show that the broad objectives discussed here are feasible. There are viable and inherently superior technologies that are more appropriate for contemporary Britain and

14

for the new quality of life age. Specifically we shall deal in more depth with the problems of energy and of establishing more small-scale manufacturing. But before this it is necessary to say something about one of the industrial catchwords of the decade — productivity.

2

Productivity: Mixing Manpower, Money and Machines

Part of modern business folklore in Britain is that the situation to be desired most is massive new investment in order to improve manpower productivity. Expressed another way, we should maximise the use of machines in order to minimise human involvement. Certainly, comparisons with other industrialised nations leave no room for doubting that there is plenty of scope in Britain to increase output per employee. However, it is seldom remarked that this objective is paradoxical in that it seeks to maximise the use of scarce financial resources, profit levels being low, whilst minimising manpower which is in plentiful supply.

Desirable as good manpower productivity is in every business, it is most important in those businesses that are manpower intensive. Furthermore, there is a danger that in focussing on this aspect of performance, management may lose sight of something which should concern them most — the overall utilisation of resources of men, money and machines. For it is a primary aim of any business to find that balanced mix of manpower and investment that will add value at minimum overall cost under the particular circumstances of the business concerned. Manpower cost minimisation does not necessarily correspond with the overall optimum use of resources as can be seen from the following comparison between BLMC(UK) and Toyota (Japan) shown on a common basis of 1 million pounds added value per annum.

	BLMC (UK)	Toyota (Japan)
Added Value per annum	£1.000m	£1.000m
Manpower Cost	£0.880m	£0.460m
Depreciation (10 year)	£0.061m	£0.108m
Investment cost @ 20% per annum	£0.135m	£0.604m
Total cost per annum	£1.076m	£1.172m

Despite the fact that manpower costs for BLMC were nearly double those of Toyota, the combined manpower and financial costs were lower in BLMC than in Toyota for a notional 20% per annum return on investments. Of course, this does not mean that with the particular mix of manpower and investment that may exist at any given time, manpower costs should not be minimised. It simply warns that there is no point in reducing the manpower cost element if it can only be achieved at an increased level of investment that is greater than the manpower cost saving. A productive company is one that adds value at a low overall cost of resources.

Underlying the belief that movement in the direction of increased capital intensiveness is the road to success is an unconscious conviction that the range of options in a country like Britain is very narrow if a company is to remain competitive. The comparison between BLMC and Toyota illustrates that the spectrum of choice may be very wide — even in the automotive industry. Moreover, it is important to consider how much more difficult it can be to obtain a satisfactory return on investment if a capital intensive option is chosen. Providing that overall productivity of men, money and machines is satisfactory, the manpower intensive operation can produce much better returns. Furthermore, the company with a low level of fixed capital invested is in a very favourable position to survive profitably through a trade recession and is often in much better shape to cope with changes in the market and competition. It is frequently the case that much of the plant in a modern capital intensive operation is very specialised and that consequently it is inflexible in its application. Firms in the car industry lead a very precarious existence when the launching of a new model involves investments of hundreds of millions of pounds at very great risk. From the narrow viewpoint of the shareholders' interest there is often good reason for management to seek out an effective resource mix which errs in the direction of labour intensiveness.

A profitable organisation is a condition of survival but a manager's task is not simply one of safeguarding the shareholders interest. It is to balance the interests of employees, suppliers, shareholders and the wider community in meeting the needs of customers. In considering these competing interests when choosing an appropriate mix of manpower and other resources, management faces a variety of important questions. For purposes of illustration, consider a major modernisation proposal which involves a big capital investment and a substantial reduction in manpower. From the point of view of employees the co-operation which management will seek in order to take advantage of the new investment will have to be bought through higher rates of pay. This will be the case whether or not any additional effort or skill is called for from employees. Indeed, a new investment more often than not requires less effort and skill; nevertheless the price has to be paid because, as a matter of principle, organised labour requires to maintain or improve its share of any wealth that is created in the company in which it is employed. Consequently a very false picture will be obtained if an inadequate allowance is made for increased pay rates. In contemplating the consequences for employment, management will have to decide whether it is better that a higher proportion of added value should go to financial interests rather than to the workforce, and whether unions will be prepared to permit an erosion of their share in added value. A closer look at the BLMC figures provides an example. Is it better that over 80% of the added value should go to the company workforce as it does at present or is it preferable that more than 60% should go to financial interests as in the case of Toyota. Managers will also have to decide whether it is better that a smaller number of people should receive increased pay whilst others lose their jobs — assuming unions would be prepared to accept such demanning. When alternative employment opportunities are plentiful this is not such a serious problem but when they are few it is a very serious matter for management, employees and the wider community. In such circumstances, if a viable alternative mix involving a bigger workforce existed, management might well be considered negligent in selecting a capital intensive option.

Managements are increasingly being forced to recognise that they are in many senses trustees of resources committed to their charge. They are realising more and more that a company is part of a wider community and good managers must try to strike a balance between the interests of employees, shareholders and the community. A choice which neglects the interests of the community is becoming unacceptable. A major investment may be entirely acceptable to shareholders and employees and yet be counter-productive for both local and national interests. The local community may suffer because a smaller proportion of the wealth created will be retained in the neighbourhood with consequent loss to local trade. Furthermore, there may be a devaluation of the local resources of skilled labour as skilled people are displaced. This can be a real loss since, basically, the true wealth of a community lies in the skills of its people. The national community may also suffer losses that are both real and financial. If a substantial component of any new capital equipment has to be imported then in effect the foreign manpower used in its manufacture would be replacing the local labour displaced and this must have an effect on our balance of payments. Other problems may arise where, since only certain parts of the economy have the potential to become highly capital intensive, this can create abnormally high rates of pay and serious problems may result in other parts of the economy. Some labour intensive activities in the services sector may be put out of business. Other possible adverse consequences exist when alternative product employment for redundant personnel is not available. Here the manpower cost saving to the company is transferred to the exchequer as lost tax revenues and

18

increased social payments. Thus a net total resource cost saving to the company may well be a net increase for the nation almost equal to the additional investment cost.

In the earlier stages of economic development an increase in capital investment was almost always beneficial to all parties. But the present situation is very much more complex and it is only by careful and unprejudiced examination of all the possible consequences that any company can find that special mix of men, money and machines which will ensure commercial success through the appropriate use of all resources.

At any level of average earnings there is a limit to manpower productivity below which there is insufficient generation of added value to cover both manpower and finance costs. At the other end of the spectrum labour productivity can be increased by investment up to a point at which the extra cost of investment is greater than the savings in manpower costs. Between this lower and upper limit there is a fairly wide range of mixtures of men, money and machines that can be used in a particular economy to create wealth. No one mix is inherently superior to another, but in many respects a mix containing a considerable manpower element has important advantages. The extreme limits may change as a result of technical developments and it is a particular objective of the appropriate technology movement to find ways of achieving high productivity with the best possible use of available human skill.

Incredibly, we hear constantly from government and opposition alike and from both sides of industry the chorus that all we need is a surge of investment in our capital-intensive industries for unemployment to decline. But in the Shell Company since the end of the war investment increased steadily until in 1975 it exceeded £1 billion. During that time production capacity and sales increased about eightfold and yet employment decreased from over 200,000 to less than 170,000. The oil industry may be exceptional but which of our big industries has such high productivity and is growing so fast that further investment will result in significantly more employment? Many industries already suffer from over-manning and to increase this would be counterproductive.

Great faith is held in the over-spill effect of job creation, i.e. the secondary jobs created by the economic activity of the larger industries. But many of these supply and service industries are themselves already over-manned. In a recent address the chairman of Shell said:

"No doubt there is some truth in this spill-over theory and certainly I hope so but in my personal opinion we are already enjoying much of the spill-over effect and I remain doubtful whether, even with renewed growth, the supply industries as a whole will engage large numbers of additional people. The whole North Sea oil and gas business — the biggest fillip to industrial activity here since the war — is now providing something like a quarter of all private fixed investment in Britain. In terms of employment it has brought some 25,000 jobs in direct employment and indirectly maybe 100,000 more; 125,000 valuable new jobs but where could you hope to find another such opportunity?''

In our low growth situation unemployment could get progressively worse for many years to come unless the labour surplus to the needs of the big capital-intensive companies can find alternative employment in new small manufacturing firms. The need for development of such new employment opportunities all over the country could not be clearer nor more urgent.

PRODUCTIVITY: Many with little or few with much?

It makes no sense to discuss *productivity* only in terms of output per employee whilst ignoring the input of capital investment. What point is there in achieving savings in labour costs if these can only be obtained at the expense of greater capital investment costs? When we are told — as we frequently are — that a Japanese worker is at least twice as productive as a British worker, what does this really mean? The data below shows that although we may use many more people and much less capital to create £1 million of added value, British industry with very similar 'gross earnings' per employee generates a somewhat better return on its capital investment than does Japan.

	UK Companies (1976) — excluding BSC	Japanese Companies —416 (1974)
Employees	6.89m	2.4m
Assets	£50,500m	£67,000m
Sales	£9,360m per employee	£26,743 per employee
Added Value (AV)	£4,893 ,, ,,	£ 7,386 ,, ,,
Assets	£7,330 ,, ,,	£27,994 ,, ,,
Gross Earnings	£3,489 ,, ,,	£ 3,471 ,, ,,
AV £1,000m	(Assets £1.500m)	(Assets £3.800m)
Manpower Costs	£0.713m	£0.477m
Depreciation	£0.092m	£0.149m
Finance costs	£0.195m — 13% pretax yield	£0.374m — 10% pretax yield
Total	£1.000m	£1.000m

From these figures it can only be concluded that with the British mix of labour and investment there is a superior utilisation of resources. The picture looks even more favourable to Britain if a realistic view is taken of what represents an acceptable level of return on investment under inflation. If Japanese companies are more competitive it would appear to be the result of things other than greater overall productivity. Of course, it is a personal judgement whether it is better as in Britain for over 70% of added value to go to employees rather than financial interest or for under 50% as is the case of Japan.

3

Energy: Cure or Prevention

Total national expenditure on energy in 1977 was £16 thousand million, a cost of about £800 per annum per household. Some idea of the significance of this figure is that it is about three times the total value of the output of the nation's agriculture and fishing industries, or about one-third of the total sales value of the country's manufacturing output, and not far short of half the total personal wealth creation of industry.

It is often thought that there exists a simple linear relationship between energy consumption and Gross Domestic Product. Whilst in a crude sense this is true, there are significant differences between countries. The accompanying figure shows the energy consumption of a number of countries as measured in tons of oil equivalent per capita. It can be seen that for any given level of GDP, some countries consume anything up to twice as much energy as others. Britain is one such country. Germany, Sweden and Denmark have GDPs roughly double that of the UK but consume about the same amount of energy per capita. Italy with a GDP similar to ours consumes about half as much energy per capita. The graph divides countries into two groups — the high and the low energy users.

Although countries are never strictly comparable in this way because of climatic and other differences, it is clear that there is scope for real savings in energy in the UK.

Since many of the low energy using European countries are themselves engaged in programmes to reduce their own consumption by about 20%, it would seem that a halving of our own use should be a realistic target. We could, therefore, be saving over £8 thousand million a year — more than the national education budget.

It is clear that if energy consumption continues at its present rate, a rapidly increasing shortage will develop here and throughout the world as oil and gas start to decline. It is generally agreed that a massive investment and construction programme is needed now if this energy

NATIONAL PER CAPITA ENERGY CONSUMPTION v GNP

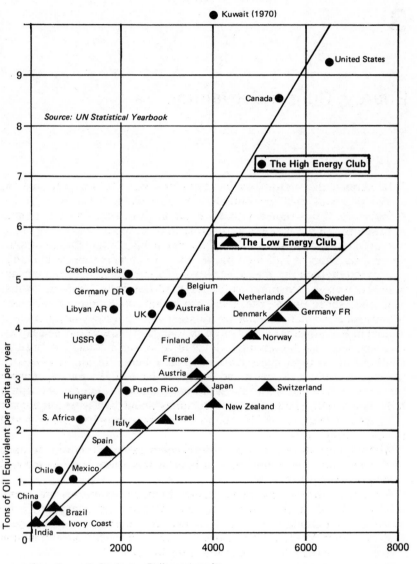

Source: UN Statistical Yearbook

gap is to be filled and there is current debate about whether this large-scale programme should be primarily nuclear or non-nuclear. The hazards and difficulties of each need no repeating. But in the long run it may be that the economic consequences of trying to replace cheap fossil fuels with more expensive energy forms will be the most serious. Not only would annual revenue costs be much greater but the share of capital formation necessary for energy investment would be much higher — perhaps prohibitatively so. If it is not to be at the expense of other things, the extra costs of this energy would have to be paid for through increased economic activity, and the production of more goods and services but this would itself be adding to the energy bill. By trying to fill the energy gap we should, in fact, be increasing our energy consumption and in view of our poor record in improving productivity, it seems highly unlikely that we could even maintain our present living standards. Pursuing this strategy would be like running faster and faster in order to stay where we are and would be questionable even if no alternative were available. But in view of the prodigious waste in our present system a very real alternative is available — the reduction of our energy consumption by 50% to bring it down to around 2 tons of oil equivalent per capita per year.

Reducing Energy Consumption

Where should we look for these potential savings in energy consumption? In summary:

- *Domestic use* accounts for around 30% of our primary energy consumption, about 75% of which is used for space heating. A serious insulation programme for the existing housing stock combined with much higher insulation standards on new housing could halve this requirement.

- *Industrial, commercial and agricultural use* accounts for about 50% of primary consumption mostly in industry, about 75% of which is used for the production of materials. A three fold increase in the life time expectancy of durables combined with extensive repair, renovation, re-use and materials recycling would, together with conventional energy conservation techniques, more than halve this requirement.

- *Transport* accounts for about 15% of primary consumption with an average efficiency of less than 20%. Road vehicles account for about 90% and about 60% of this is for cars. There is good reason to believe that mileage per gallon could be doubled. Furthermore, we transport only about 15% of freight by rail in this country compared with 50% in the USA, Japan and most Western European countries. Transfer of a substantial proportion of this freight to rail could halve fuel consumption since rail is up to three times as energy efficient as road transport.

23

— *Military and other uses* account for about 5% of primary consumption.

We can discuss these potentials for energy saving in more detail. It could be maintained that, as a result of pre-occupation with cosmetic innovation and fashion changes, the architectural profession has lost sight of one of the fundamental purposes of a building — to provide economically comfortable shelter and protection for the occupants from the variable conditions of the local climate. Whereas in earlier times the structure of a building played a dominant role in maintaining a relatively even internal temperature, with heating playing only a minor part, following the introduction of new active heating systems the passive role of the building itself has been neglected. As a consequence we now have houses and other buildings with inferior thermal properties equipped with space heating systems that are very costly to operate because their energy output is so readily radiated to outer space. Neglect of the thermal function of the building structure has resulted in the creation of the radiant house which, instead of maximising the benefit from solar radiation for internal space heating, uses prodigious quantities of irreplaceable fossil fuels to heat the atmosphere.

The average cost of home space heating in Britain amounts to about 5% of annual household expenditure i.e. about £150 per annum. It is widely recognised that a reduction of between one-third and one-half of space heating fuel consumption is possible by means of insulating existing housing stock. This would represent savings to each household of between £50 and £75 annually. Such savings would be sufficient to pay the costs of a high level of insulation well within 10 years. Of course, for the remaining life of the building there would be no further charges to offset against the savings. Furthermore, since space heating requirements are for low grade heat sources (under 100°C) additional savings on primary energy can be made by the development of a variety of heat technology options including:—

— waste heat sources such as combined heat and power systems;
— solar systems including the use of solar walls, roofs and panels;
— heat pumps etc.

The combination of these alternative low grade heat sources with insulation programmes could probably achieve the required reduction in primary energy consumption by around 50%. It should also be remembered that the same principles apply to the space heating of industrial, commercial and public facilities. These together with domestic use presently account for 40% of primary energy consumption.

The greatest consumption of primary energy occurs in the industrial and commercial sectors: agriculture consumes less than 5%. Roughly 75% of industrial energy is used in the production of basic materials and only about 25% in the transformation of those materials into finished products. For this reason it was emphasised earlier that the greatest potential for reducing energy consumption in production lies

24

in the manufacture of long-life goods instead of the low first cost, throw-away articles much emphasised at present. Longer life articles could reduce primary energy need by two or three times, as one product replaced the two or three required over the same time period at present. Through the parallel development of the repair and reconditioning businesses, energy would be effectively traded for manpower. The various other advantages of the life cost approach to product manufacture, including more satisfying and geographically dispersed work opportunities and reductions in material consumption, were discussed in the first part of this paper.

Three events provide some encouraging signs of a changing attitude towards the long-life motor car. The Loughborough University of Technology has an on-going research project looking at matching the commercial feasibility of the long-life car to feasible ideas on design and manufacture. The Porsche company has undertaken its own research on a long-life vehicle and one of the main reasons for the Design Council Award to Ford for the 'Fiesta' was the attention paid in the design to facilitating maintenance and repair.

Despite growing public disaffection with the dominance of heavy road vehicles for freight transportation, road transport remorselessly increases its share of the UK freight market and vehicles increase in numbers, size and mileage covered. Between 1962 and 1972 the total tonnage of goods consumed increased by slightly more than 20%, but the tonnage of goods transported increased by 25% and the number of ton-miles increased by nearly 33%. During the same period both the tonnage and the ton-miles contributed by rail, shipping and inland waterways decreased and more than the whole of the overall national increase was consequently taken up by road transport with a massive increase of 70% in road ton-miles. By 1972 more than 85% of all goods transported in Britain travelled by road and the tonnage carried by rail fell below 10%.

There is widespread feeling that these trends are an inevitable consequence of economic growth. As consumption grows so the weight of goods carried must increase proportionally, and as industry becomes more centralised so each ton will inevitably need to be carried greater distances. That an increasing proportion of this is carried by road vehicles is merely a consequence of road transport being the most modern, efficient, flexible and cheapest system.

Undoubtedly from the point of view of an individual business, there is considerable attraction in a single mode, door-to-door transfer by road. But from a national point of view there are other considerations not least of which concerns the extent to which the use of roads by heavy goods transport is being subsidised by the taxpayer. There are also social and environmental factors involved in considering the balance between road and rail freight transportation. One important factor concerns the appalling toll of road accidents and deaths.

Between 1962 and 1971 there were 1 million serious accidents and deaths on the roads and it is estimated that something in the order of 10 million people suffered serious anxiety because a member of the family was seriously injured. There is a 20—1 greater chance of serious accidents in road transport than in rail. Of course medical services can do little about the deaths and more serious disabilities so caused but the costs to the nation of trying i.e. of maintaining accident and emergency services, intensive care units and rehabilitation services are in effect another form of subsidy to all road transport users.

As far as energy is concerned, road vehicles operate at low efficiency levels of less than 20%. Energy consumption per ton mile by road vehicle is between two and three times that by rail and major energy savings could be achieved through a more intensive use of rail for freight transport.

Electricity
Approximately one-third of all primary fuel used in Britain is for the generation of electricity. This in itself results in tremendous waste since the overall thermal efficiency of the central electricity generating and grid distribution system is only 25%. Thus for every four tons of coal burned in power stations, three are used to heat the atmosphere and only one is useful to the consumer. Much of this inefficiency can be attributed to the policy of having very big and remotely-sited power stations in place of the previous small local stations. Not only were transmission losses smaller than with the present system but also the use of power station waste heat for space heating of industrial and domestic buildings was much more feasible. There are numerous examples in European cities in which a local combined heat and power station provides electricity and space heating requirements through district heating systems with an overall thermal efficiency of 75-85%. Instead of three out of every four tons of fuel being used to heat the atmosphere, only one ton in four is wasted in these systems. In several major Swedish cities more than two thirds of the buildings are heated by the local power station waste heat.

Not only do we produce electricity inefficiently but consumption per capita in Britain is substantially higher than in other Western European countries. This is partially explained by the extent to which we use electricity for space heating purposes. To illustrate the magnitude involved, it has been estimated that if all domestic electric heating was done by gas there would be an annual saving of 18 million tons of coal and a capital saving of about £1,000 million.

Given this tremendous scope for reduced electricty use and increased efficiency in the use of primary fuel, potentially enormous energy savings are possible given a sufficiently determined national programme. Such debate as presently exists is, however, focussed mainly on the problem of electricity supply with most emphasis on the pros and cons of nuclear power. If it were decided that not only should we discontinue with our present excessive use of electricity but that we should also change our wasteful centralised generating system, then the overall requirement for generating capacity and the fuel required for it would be so substantially reduced that the nuclear power problem might no longer be a real issue. If we could eliminate the need for additional capacity there would be no need to worry about what kind of capacity to build.[1]

One further point might be noted under the general heading of energy. We have seen that the potential savings from the elimination of wasted energy are very large. Who then will benefit from these savings? Everyone is likely to gain to some extent but it may not be too much to hope that the poorer sections of the community may feel some real benefit. Since wasted energy costs the average family about £400 per annum, it can be seen that a redirection of energy savings to the poorest 25%, for example, would provide them with around £1,600 a year extra.

However, the realistic possibility of implementing redistribution policies favouring the poorer social groups remains a matter of conjecture. Pay differentials exist in all societies, and, in most cases about two-thirds of the population have incomes close to the national average whilst the remaining third is divided about equally between those with income substantially higher or lower than the average. It is not difficult to see how, in a democratic society, political will can be mobilised to reduce the share enjoyed by those with substantially higher than average incomes. The small minority of high income earners have little possibility of resisting the wishes of the majority who stand to benefit from such a redistribution. But the same political consensus works against redistribution for the benefit of the poor. The massive majority do not wish to see their hard-won gains given to the poorest minority when they are evidently receiving incomes or social payments not that much less than their own. Anyone who has taken part in a Christian Aid or other charity door-to-door collection knows how many people on average British earnings or even higher see themselves as part of the poor.

In fact between 1949 and 1976 there was a dramatic fall in the share going to the 10% of highest income earners whilst little significant change occurred in the share taken by those with low incomes. In fact, over a period of economic growth it is in some ways remarkable that the share going to those with low incomes did not significantly decline. Perhaps in some measure the degree of stability achieved owes something to the acceptance of moderate redistribution policies that did not go so far as to erode the share of the majority.

It is probably too much to hope that savings in our waste bill can

27

be effectively directed to the poor — though this should not stop us attempting to do so. But even if the value of savings on energy and everything else amounted to no more than, say, £200 on a poor family's budget the real benefit may be far greater than is likely to be obtained from income redistribution policies.

Note
1. Some encouragement comes with the announcement by the Central Electricity Generating Board Chairman, that they are now examining schemes for building small coal fired power stations on the sites of the old small city generating stations that are scheduled for closure.

4

Small Enterprises: From Decline to Revival

As a nation we are passing through a period which in the future may be seen in retrospect as a turning point in our commercial, industrial and economic affairs. That which is inappropriate in the old system is breaking down and will continue to decay. Most of our highly centralised and excessively complex large institutions are not appropriate to these changing times and they lack the flexibility to adapt. It makes no sense to artificially extend the life of such institutions nor of the narrow concepts of organisation and technologies on which they are based. We must now build in a more decentralised and less complex way to steadily replace the old system and a central component of this reconstruction must be the encouragement of new, small enterprises.

For the past twenty years there has been a serious deficiency in the creation of these small new growth centres. In the manufacturing sector alone this has resulted in a loss of more than 1.5 million jobs over a period during which most other advanced industrial nations have increased employment in industry. As a consequence Britain has become increasingly dependent upon imports of manufactured goods, mainly from countries that have a flourishing and innovatory small firm sector.

This is not to say, however, that the only technologies which are appropriate for the future are those which can be successfully employed in small enterprises, but the trend should be to do as much as possible on a small-scale and in geographically dispersed units. In many industries, economies of scale have been grossly over-estimated whilst many externalities have been completely ignored. There can be little doubt that a great deal of what is presently done in big factories in Britain could be done better in much smaller units with, in addition, many social, environmental and resource economy benefits.

Reasons for Decline
Comparison with other industrialised countries at two levels of size

shows how badly the UK has suffered in the contraction of its small manufacturing sector. Whereas in this country less than 30% of manufacturing employment is in plants of less than 200 employees, in France, Japan and Sweden the proportion is 50% or more. At the smallest level of less than 10 employees there are only about 27,000 manufacturers in this country compared with 180,000 in France and 150,000 in Germany. Furthermore, the difference is getting rapidly worse, with a considerably higher 'death rate' and a 'birth rate' of only about one-third of some other industrial countries.

A number of reasons can be identified which account for the abnormal rates of closure and opening of small enterprises in Britain:

— Unrestricted take-over of some small firms by big ones followed by closure of the small firms.
— Small-firm failures consequent upon a high level of closures of big firms whom they served.
— A decline of repair and renovation businesses resulting from labour costs inflated by high taxation of incomes.
— Forced closure of many small businesses as a result of indiscriminate redevelopment of inner-city areas and unfavourable zoning policies.
— Unfavourable and very cyclic economic and trading conditions in the country.
— An exceptional burden of legislation which does not discriminate between big and small companies and which is particularly restrictive on small-company operation.
— Planning policies detrimental to the interests of small businesses and a lack of very small workshops for starters.
— An increase in business financial risks associated with reduced profit potential and many softer options for earning a good living.
— High income taxes which have seriously limited the availability of private risk capital.
— The return on other investments (property, fixed interest stock) has been better and with far less risk involved for the institutional investors, who have become the dominant trustees of private wealth.
— Loan interest rates have been and are exceptionally high in this country.
— Very damaging long-supply credit practices exist which are especially to the detriment of small businesses.
— Excessively favourable purchase terms for raw materials and components are available to big companies which places smaller ones at an unfair disadvantage.
— Relatively high taxes on income at all levels have put British businesses at a serious international competitive disadvantage, especially in the more manpower-intensive small companies.
— High rates of corporation tax have restricted small companies

with very limited credit-worthiness from investing in better equipment out of retained earnings.

— A steadily increasing bureaucratic burden has been placed on all businesses which is particularly damaging to small ones.

— Commerce and industry have been called upon to bear a higher proportion of rates. This together with high rents has been disastrous to many companies in highly rated inner cities.

— Self-employed people are discriminated against on NHI payments and benefits.

— High inflation rates are especially difficult for a small and impecunious company to deal with.

— There is an unfavourable attitude towards industry and commerce in society at large and in educational circles in particular. Business has consequently been starved of the able and enterprising people that are needed to set up and run successful companies.

In any society where the buyer has freedom to choose between alternative goods and services it is certain that every firm born will, if it survives the first very vulnerable few years, go through a process of growth, maturity, decline and closure. As in the rest of the natural world this is a healthy and stable state so long as the growth is cellular rather than monolithic. Throughout most of this century and certainly since the Second World War, conditions have been created in Britain favouring the development of industrial giants, which progressively have had to be subjected to increasing surveillance and control as some of these companies reached a near monopoly position. However, Britain has not developed legislation (comparable with the US anti-trust laws for example) in order to prevent practices that restrict competition and to give protection to small firms. Regretably, whilst mainly intended to apply to big firms, the controls which have been imposed for the benefit of employees, the consumer and society at large have universal application and have been very damaging to small companies.

The Need to Favour Small Firms

The Report of the Committee of Inquiry (the Bolton Committee) published in 1971 advocated that there need not be discrimination in favour of small firms but prescribed steps that should be taken to remove the inequities and disabilities which small firms suffer. Since then there has certainly been no move in favour of small firms — quite the contrary in fact as more resources are channelled from public funds into big companies in both the private and public sectors — and there is little sign of the inequities and disabilities being removed. It now seems quite clear that unless there is a loosening of shackles and positive steps are taken to support small firms — particularly embryo enterprises during the first five years of life — there is unlikely to be any revival in the small business sector with all that this can mean in terms of further narrowing of our manufacturing base.

31

There are many other pressing claims for Government assistance and no priority is likely to be given merely on the basis that it is needed. The justification for priority to be given to small firms is doubly compelling. Firstly, the future of the public service sector depends entirely upon the creation of wealth by agriculture, industry and commerce. At the present time Government spending is equal to more than 50% of Gross Domestic Product and revenue claims more than 40% of all value added — the difference being covered by borrowing. The Government and society generally has a big vested interest, therefore, in assisting the generation of additional added value from which it can derive revenue. Thus assistance to new enterprises, whether financial or in any other form, is not in any sense an altruistic act on the part of Government. It is a matter of vital self-interest. Without the creation of these new sources of wealth, society will be unable to enjoy the various services which have been developed. Viewed at another level, it is a matter of social justice that those who are taking very great personal and family risks in setting up new enterprises should not be required to bear the whole of that risk when the State takes nearly half of the fruits of the enterprise at no risk to itself. If the Government were to diminish the entrepreneurial risk in proportion to its share in value added there would be a substantial inducement to people to set up new businesses and an extension of social justice to this section of society which up to now has been grossly exploited.

A second and now urgent justification is that the small-firm sector promises a greater potential for the creation of useful employment at minimum cost than any other section of the economy. By comparison with other Government initiatives to reduce unemployment, discrimination in favour of the small-firm sector would be very cost effective.

What Discrimination is Required?
From the long list of reasons given above for the abnormally high rate of decline in the British small-manufacturing sector it is to be expected that a fairly wide range of changes will be required if the trend is to be reversed. Many changes will need to be implemented both by central and local government action. These will be discussed first. There are, however, other non-governmental actions which could give added impetus to a revival of small-scale enterprises and these will be mentioned subsequently.

i) *Exempt all manufacturers employing less than 20 people from most of the restrictive legislation and bureaucratic interference that has been introduced during the past thirty years.*
No doubt it will be argued by some that such a step would mean a return of undesirable practices which could be harmful to many sections of

society and it cannot be denied that this will happen in some instances. The balance of interest of society in general is, however, served if this degree of freedom is restored to the small firm and the price that will be paid will be small by comparison with the advantages gained from a more vigorous small-scale sector.

The variety and range of legislation is very great and every item needs to be considered carefully. There may be some things which have little or no adverse effect on the small firm in which case there would be no point in changing the law. Other things which are more burdensome may nevertheless need to be retained because their removal would be unacceptable. For example, a requirement to provide special safety equipment when working with a seriously noxious material such as asbestos would almost certainly need to be applied to all firms no matter what their size of operation. On the other hand many other new standards that are being applied to new factories but are not obligatory for existing plant need not be applied to very small new firms.

Whilst measures which have been made to give greater protection to employees against such things as unfair dismissal and to provide compensation in the form of redundancy pay are universally welcomed, it must be appreciated that even such highly desirable laws can be ruinous to a very small firm and equally may well prevent people from setting up in business. Regrettable as it may be, the removal of such restrictions on small firms is necessary if more people are to be encouraged to take the risks of starting new firms. The application of the principle of the State safety net can surely protect small firm employees and thereby ensure that they are not discriminated against compared with fellow workers in big firms.

Alongside the mushroom growth of restrictive legislation there has been an explosion of petty bureaucratic interference most of which, at considerable cost to the taxpayer as well as to the businessman, makes no contribution to national wealth creation. On the contrary it considerably diminishes it. The stories that can be told of futile form-filling are legion. Its sole purpose appears to be to provide mountains of information for armies of statisticians, clerks, computer programmers etc. to assemble, collate, process and analyse so that if by chance you may wish to know how many cups of tea were served in British hotel bedrooms between October and December of last year you can find out — providing you can find the right department. It is sometimes said that in times of change and difficulty the middle classes are the first to find a way of taking care of their interests. Possibly the recent information explosion, which has created the fastest growing industry in the world at the present time, is the latest example of this phenomenon. Big companies can employ their own army of people to prevent their line managers having their time wasted by the perpetual stream of form-filling demands, some of which require days of work to complete. A small firm has no such opportunity and the intolerable burden falls on the shoulders of the person who may already be working 60 hours a week or more. There is only one way to deal with this problem and that is to exempt all small firms below a certain prescribed size from any official returns other than those required for tax purposes.

ii) *Remove planning restrictions on small manufacturing operations of, say, 10 people or less and make available low-rental workspace.*

One of the worst features of the thinking of town planners this century has been the dissociation of the residential community from the working community. The worst aspects of this are now to be seen in many inner city areas where residential and recreational development has gone ahead with no regard for employment. As a consequence, male unemployment rates in some inner city areas are around 20% (near Third World levels) and in London alone between 1966 and 1971, 25% of all manufacturing jobs were lost. Many of these were the direct result of redevelopment.

Most people starting a new manufacturing business require a workshop close to home. Furthermore, it needs to be very small and very cheap with security of tenure. Such facilities no longer exist in most parts of Britain and anyone attempting to trade from a garden shed or convert a small old building nearby will invariably meet opposition from planning authorities who have zoned industry in some remote estate with expensive factories usually with no less than 2,000 sq. ft. of floor area. To get started no more than 200 sq. ft. may be required.

Whatever may be the reasons for segregating big factories, there seems very little sense in prohibiting small manufacturing operations providing the occupants are subject to normal controls of public nuisance. There are very few small-scale manufacturing activities that are in any way obnoxious.

In fact many would agree that those activities that used to take place in the patchwork of town life added considerably to the colour and vitality of the community.

Well-meaning planning policies are interfering with the right and the obligation to work. But the removal of planning restrictions will not alone provide the workshops required. There also needs to be within most communities a positive policy of providing the type of small workspace that a starter needs. How this is done will obviously vary from place to place but in some towns there are fine old commercial and industrial buildings, no longer in use, which can at low cost be converted for multiple occupation by small firms. Where this can be done there are very real advantages to the occupants and with such an establishment there is a possibility of providing useful common services which can ease the very heavy burden of a small manufacturer struggling for survival.

iii) *Share the risk, by guarantee, of the seed capital required by small new firms and provide loan finance at low (subsidised) levels of interest.*
The justification for the Government to share in the very high capital risk involved in a new venture has already been explained. With present levels of revenue an equitable share would be 40% of any losses of risk capital, guaranteed to the providers of finance in the event of failure. Such an arrangement would obviate the need for State participation or surveillance. Some limits would need to be set for the operation of such a scheme. An overall limit of £50,000 Government risk would be sufficient to cover businesses with up to £125,000 risk capital. In order to encourage creation of employment another limit could also be imposed on the basis of, for example, £7,000 per employee. Thus for a firm employing only five people but having a risk capital of £125,000, the Government guarantee would be limited to £35,000 (i.e. 5 × £7,000) rather than £50,000. This overall limit would only be reached if more than seven people were employed.

Since there are virtually no traditional private sources of risk capital left for new business ventures, the entrepreneur usually has to supply his own capital and this frequently involves second mortgages on homes. The burden would be greatly eased if the Government were to subsidise and guarantee bank loans up to the limits specified above for a limited period of, say, five years, by which time those businesses that are sound will have reached a reasonably stable state and should be capable of standing on their own feet. An alternative to subsidised rates of interest might be deferred interest payments. Dr F. E. Jones of Philips Industries has, however, made out a very sound case for subsidised loan finance for all projects which are capable of adding at least £1 of value for every £1 of capital employed.*

iv) *Provide tax-free periods for new small firms*
It might be thought that guaranteeing part of the risk capital and providing low-interest finance would be sufficient incentive to anyone or any co-operative group contemplating setting up in business. However, there is nearly always a very real cash problem for new firms during the first few years, which cripples many of them despite the fact that the owners may take out an absolutely minimal income. The high rate of corporation tax (43% on profits of less than £20,000 and 52% at higher profit levels) makes it extremely difficult for a new firm to accumulate sufficient retained earnings to provide a comfortable cash position. A considerable number of unnecessary premature failures would be prevented if new small enterprises were given a short-term tax holiday for, say, the first five years. Such discrimination has been available in many countries for a long time. Our indifference to the survival of the new economic growth in our society is exceptional.

*"The Economic Ingredients of Industrial Success" *I.Mech.E.Proc.* 1976.

v) *Raise the minimum sales turnover limit for VAT*
At present the limit is set at a turnover level of £10,000, which means in effect that every business is caught in the VAT net without exception. Even the smallest one-man operation is therefore required to undertake the complex administration required by VAT authorities on every single transaction. At an 8% level of tax it is clear that no significant net benefit can be obtained by the Exchequer for very small businesses, and the cost both to the nation and the businessman is indefensible.

vi) *Remove the National Insurance surcharge on self-employed people*
Most people starting up a new firm are self-employed. In addition to a self-employed standard contribution for National Insurance of £2.66 per week, such a person is required to pay an additional 8% of earnings in excess of £1,750 p.a. up to £5,500 p.a. Thus a man or woman drawing average national earnings of about £3,500 will pay a surcharge of £140 for National Insurance, despite the fact that there is no entitlement to unemployment benefit should the business fail.

vii) *Regulate terms of trade and purchase credit terms*
The operation of terms of trade and credit payment systems in the British economy is generally unsatisfactory. They are frequently very damaging to small business firms and invariably work in favour of the wealthy and large firms.

The factors which probably put small firms at the greatest competitive disadvantage are the exceptionally favourable discounts and rebates that big and powerful firms are able to extract from their suppliers. It is frequently alleged that they are fully justified because of the large volume orders involved which require less overhead costs. In practice the level of discounts often goes well beyond any such savings as may be made, with the result that smaller purchasers are, in fact, subsidising the bigger customers. Bearing in mind that the cost of purchases usually represents 50% (or sometimes more) of the sales value of a company's output, a small premium payed by a small firm puts it immediately at a serious competitive disadvantage with a bigger one. A 10% difference in the cost of purchases (raw materials, packages and components) is equivalent to a 5% difference in sales value. In many industries manpower costs are frequently only 20% of sales value; thus a 10% discount on purchases may be the equivalent of 25% of manpower costs. In many big firms low product costs owe more to the low cost of purchases than they do to productive efficiency, and in some cases poor productivity is masked by cheap purchases. A far healthier state of competition would exist if all purchases were made at a common list price irrespective of order size. In these circumstances big firms would still enjoy such advantages as may be inherent in the scale of their operation. In any case, discounts and rebates should be restricted so that the customer gained no greater benefit than the true value to the supplier of his large volume order. This would very seldom exceed 5%. A system which automatically favours the strong and rich has within it the seeds of its own destruction.

Many small firms suffer great hardship and sometimes collapse as a result of delaying tactics practiced by big public and private organisations in paying their debts. This is a particularly unpleasant business tactic since the victim can seldom afford to take any effective self-protective action against the culprit. Legislation introducing universal direct debiting would ensure that disputes raised by the customer could be settled without an overhanging threat of non-payment for goods or services received.

viii) *Switch the burden of taxation from people to things*
The big, mass production firm is to a considerable extent the product of a system which has discouraged the employment of people by placing high taxes on personal income and has tolerated the prodigal waste of raw materials and fossil fuels by leaving them almost free of taxes. A reversal of this practice so that a great part of the revenue is raised by levying taxes on virgin raw materials (but not recycled materials) and reducing or eliminating income taxes, would do much to help re-establish long-life, high-quality products in place of the "throw-away" sort that have become common in the past thirty years. Small, manpower-intensive manufacturers would benefit directly by such a shift. There would also be greater incentives for renovation and recycling operations in such an economy, which favour the small enterprise.

ix) *Restrict the absorption of small firms by take-over*
Last but by no means least in importance there is a need to prevent further reduction of the small-firm sector as a result of acquisitions made by major industrial concerns and this requires legislation. A substantial reduction in small businesses has occurred as a result of big companies using their financial muscle to buy out and subsequently close down local firms in order to make way for their own remote operations by elimination of market competition. Very familiar examples are local bakeries and breweries. This is not asset stripping of moribund companies, it is the destruction of economically viable and socially valuable parts of local communities.

Legislation which prevents deals. the consequences of which are to diminish market competition, would go a long way towards the creation of a more favourable economic climate in this country.

Non-governmental action
It would be misleading to suggest that the only worthwhile action required to reverse the trend of decline in small manufacturing is governmental.In a free society there are many vital matters which the

government can do very little about. In the main what has been described before is a removal of impediments previously imposed by Government. A great deal more is required of society in general if a major change is to occur. The creation by those members of each community who have the desire and the will to bring about the renewal of local enterprise could be of considerable value and this is the subject studied in Chapter 5.

Identifying small business opportunities
There are many people in present day society in all walks of life and of all ages who would dearly love to set up in business. Few of them have the desire to become very rich and most recognise the improbability of ever doing so. Of course they hope they will be able to earn a decent living — hopefully better than their present one — but an equal motivation is to build something of which they can be proud.

Many of them have definite ideas of what they want to do — unfortunately the ideas are not always commercially viable. Others are eager to set up in some business or other but they are not clear about the kind of enterprise that would best suit them. This uncertainty is sometimes an indication that the person concerned may not have the necessary commitment, energy and flare to make a success of their own business but others, who do have plenty of these vital qualities, may well be able to succeed, even with a not very promising project. A good project will fail in the hands of an inadequate person but a good entrepreneur can make a winner out of an almost hopeless proposition.

There is no answer to the question "What can I do?" that anyone else can give to someone who is in search of business that they can throw themselves into — only they themselves know the answer. But their search may be helped by some systematic thinking and enquiring in their own locality. The following are some clues or signposts that a potential entrepreneur may find helpful.

Clues for choosing what NOT to do:—
Nearly all new businesses start very small and cannot afford to pay for outside professional services. Whatever you choose to do, you will personally need to be capable of undertaking all the many different tasks that are involved. You may not have to do everything all the time but you must be able to when the need arises. This is the first and most important factor limiting the choice of business you can set up. It will still leave most people with many alternatives, but these personal factors are all important.

It is customers that make a business. The search for a good business prospect is in the main a matter of identifying a customer or customers (or slice of a market) with needs for either goods or a service which a newcomer can satisfy in some way or other better than — or at least as well as — existing businesses. Look for the market first, then see what sort of business will be suitable. Too many people are obsessed with their product or service idea and only see the customer as incidental.

All commercial enterprise is about adding value through the application of human skill and energy to whatever material or information resources that the business takes in. (The window cleaning company produces an output of income from cleaned windows by the application of skill and energy to a bucket of water, a leather and a ladder.) For survival, the value added (i.e. sales revenue minus total cost of all purchased materials and services) must substantially exceed all the money taken out in wages, National Insurance, pension contributions etc. Not many businesses can survive for long if the value added is less than 1.5 times the manpower costs. This rough rule of thumb test will eliminate a good many non-starter ideas.

There are some activities for which big companies are well suited and some which are best handled by small firms. Avoid trying to compete with big firms in those things they do well but remember that sometimes big firms mistakenly try to do things which do not really suit them and in these cases a small firm will succeed in competition.

Avoid businesses in which customers require long credit terms and suppliers give little credit.

Avoid businesses where the value added per unit sold is very low. These usually require a large volume turnover at all times.

Except where services are the commodity on sale, the cost of purchased materials and services will usually amount to between a half and two-thirds of the sales revenue. Be careful not to choose a business where you are going to be at a serious disadvantage as a result of the small discounts and rebates available to you by comparison with the larger ones available to your competitors, unless there is some other substantial cost advantage to offset it (e.g. very low delivery or overhead costs).

Avoid becoming too closely dependent on customers who are either in a dying activity or are subjected to abnormally big ups and downs in their trade.

Signposts for choosing what to do:—
In modern society there are many gaps in the provision of most services. Frequently, charges are high and service is often both slow and unsatisfactory. There are many opportunities for competent services, efficiently run and with rapid response; particularly in repair and maintenance, where these are carried out at repair centres with customers providing delivery and collection.

We live in a society in which change is rapid. Look for opportunities of getting in on the early stages of a new trend (e.g. a new generation of electronic read-out petrol pumps on service stations). This will help your growth towards becoming a stable and mature business. Large parts of our material system are old and worn and in need of renovation and modernisation. There are many opportunities for small firms to take part.

In the past 15 years imports of manufactured goods for our own requirements have increased from 20% to nearly 60%, mostly from countries with much higher labour costs than Britain and a great deal from small manufacturing firms. Look around and see how many simple things are no longer made in Britain. With the market on your doorstep and relatively modest labour rates, there are a myriad of opportunities in which you will have a head start over foreign suppliers.

At any moment there are plenty of opportunities to make or sell under licence from both home and foreign firms or to enter into franchise arrangements.

Our mass production society flourishes on standardisation, and on high volume manufacture of a limited range of sizes and designs. Non-standard items (sizes, colours, designs) can still be supplied by small firms on a small batch basis.

The short life span of many 'durable' articles presents problems in the supply of spares for obsolete items. Small firms can meet that need.

Slow and uncertain delivery has become fairly widespread in Britain. Many opportunities can be identified where this is a serious problem (e.g. order books of some small furniture manufacturers are as much as two years behind). Reliable and rapid delivery combined with consistent quality is a recipe for success.

Through the decline in the small firms sector many major firms have been forced increasingly to depend upon supplies and services provided from a considerable distance — often overseas. A newcomer in the district may be able to do the job more satisfactorily.

New materials are frequently developed by manufacturers, many of which present exceptional opportunities for people wanting to produce new products, or old products with a distinct design or value for money.

Many big firms regularly purify their product ranges eliminating small volume items which customers can no longer obtain. These may sometimes provide a basis for a small specialist business.

Some Special Opportunity Categories:—
The affluent society is tiring of the uniformity of mass produced designs and there are rapidly growing opportunities for higher quality, craft or semi-craft products.

DIY activities are one of the fastest growth sectors of our economy and of other industrial nations, providing ample opportunities in the supply of goods and services at a local level.

The throw-away society produces mountains of waste products of all sorts with very low scrap value. This provides a wide range of opportunities with great potential:—

Reconditioning of machines/equipment/components
Re-upholstery
Furniture renovation
Building renovation and modernisation
Nearly-new clothing stores
Design and manufacture of machines using scrap components
Products made from waste materials
Waste materials recycling operations
Minimum packaging products

Purchase of some second-hand goods is now becoming more fashionable.

In a world of rapidly increasing material and energy costs, short-life articles are becoming too costly for many people to own or replace. There are growing opportunities for long-life durables goods supplied on a rental basis.

There is increasing concern with and regulation of all sorts of environmental pollution, safety and health at work and waste disposal. These all have produced many new small business opportunities.

Recent big increases in transport costs have put some long distance delivery systems at a disadvantage and favour the revival of small local production. Bakeries are an example.

Some of the large number of small local business premises which were closed following take-over or which otherwise stopped trading, are still unoccupied. These unused local properties provide opportunities for new firms.

The energy crisis has opened up a great many new possibilities for small new businesses. They fall broadly into two categories:—

i) energy saving (e.g. building insulation, heating and lighting control systems, total energy schemes, district heating schemes, waste heat utilisation systems, energy storage schemes etc.)

ii) alternative energy systems (e.g. heat pumps, wind machines, wood burning stoves, water power units, solar panels, solar electric cells etc.)

Recent commodity price changes and other considerations have revived possibilities of processing and using local natural materials (natural fibres, stone, timber, clay etc.) and other natural local resources (waterpower, wind, sun).

Developments in electronics (microprocessors etc.) are producing a revolution in many technologies. They are of very great importance in saving energy and materials through replacement of expensive and complicated mechanical systems and in the contribution that they can make towards miniaturisation and the operation of small-scale, dispersed activities.

Weaknesses and shortcomings have developed in many parts of the public service system, some of which present opportunities for new, local, private, commercial initiatives with worthwhile social potential.

In the field of private transport there is a revival in cycling.

Growing interest in physical exercise and recreation is producing new commercial opportunities.

An increasing part of the population is developing a wide range of taste for foreign foods and drink, which provides opportunities for local production.

5

Local Enterprises Trusts:
A Community Approach

As we move into the post-industrial age the recovery by a large section of the population of a belief in their own abilities to satisfy the needs of their families and their neighbours — the belief that they are part of a community — is perhaps the most valuable prize to be gained. The technologies that we take with us into this age will only be appropriate if they can overcome the causes of concern discussed in the first chapter of this paper i.e. if they are environmentally sound, energy and resource efficient, create more meaningful work and converging social interests. One ingredient in our future ways of doing things must be the small enterprise.

The previous chapter touched upon some of the reasons for the decline in Britain's small firms, mentioned some of the conditions that local and central Government should create to assist the necessary revival of this sector and concluded that not all the changes required can come from Government. Often, communities themselves must take the initiative. Smaller, decentralised and 'home grown' enterprises can help to overcome the currently widespread feelings of personal dependence on large, complex private and public firms and organisations, and can help to recreate self-reliance. Whilst the growth of small firms will not automatically guarantee the development of appropriate technologies, it will provide the opportunity for more people to become involved in what local manufacturing makes, how it is made and who makes it. The potential gains of this opportunity can be maximised if communities are actively involved and if ownership relations can be developed to encourage individual commitment to the success of productive ventures.

Small firms in themselves are not the whole answer and new institutional vehicles are necessary for the effective and progressive introduction of appropriate technologies throughout society. Because of the very nature of appropriate technologies these institutions must be local and co-operative. Somehow the new institutions that we are seeking must be able to combine an entrepreneurial function with a social responsibility. They should be entrepreneurial in the sense that they are concerned with wealth creating and must therefore be self-supporting. They should also be broadly based community institutions credible to all sections of the local community and not dominated by any single or group interest. For this reason the institutions themselves should not be profit-distributing. They also have an educational function since the development of appropriate technologies is inevitably involved in changing the balance of power in society and they must be seen not only to be enterprising but also to be acting for the social good. Initially, institutions for appropriate technologies should not be started on too ambitious a scale. A strong and healthy organisation is most likely to evolve if its growth is slow and based upon its own achievements and increasing credibility in its community. No attempt should be made to create rapid change by heavy injections of money or any other 'sledge hammer' tactics in order to provide quick (but probably unstable) solutions to problems such as unemployment. Although there would be advantages in creating a national link network to support institutions with services and the cross fertilisation of experience, the temptation to create a standardised model should be resisted. Each local institution should be purpose built to match local needs, resources and potentialities, and should be free to experiment. Probably the most valuable role for the new institutions, at least initially, is that of fostering small local enterprises that offer the potential to apply appropriate technology principles whilst at the same time encouraging the extention of the appropriate technology approach in all individual firms wherever this is feasible.

Local Enterprise Trusts
Against the background of these broad objectives and for many other special local reasons, groups of responsible people in many parts of the country are trying to create community based organisations in order to assist in a variety of ways with the revival of a home-grown, small business sector. In some instances major local industrial companies are co-operating and some are even taking the initiative. These organisations are trying to provide the means of reducing the risks and lightening the burdens of new starters and of helping small existing firms overcome problems that threaten their survival.

Such organisations, which have become known as Local Enterprise Trusts, have a variety of different constitutional and legal forms but in essence they are non-profit making and are fulfilling an important social function in promoting the economic well-being of the local community. They serve a wide range of interests and for the most part are able to call upon a wide range of resources. Although they usually work closely with local Government and other insitutions they are essentially local groups and are independent and autonomous entities. A kind of informal working definition has been adopted by many of these groups as follows:

"A Local Enterprise Trust is a broadly based local group involved in the creation of worthwhile work through the fostering and development of small enterprises.

It functions primarily by helping with access to technical and professional assistance and information and by promoting collaborative arrangements as in, for example, marketing and the provision of premises. It is a non-profit distributing organisation which may (or may not) establish trading subsidiaries in pursuit of its primary ends."

In many separate localities this broad description has been interpreted in various organisational forms as a result of careful study of what is needed in order to assist the development and reduce the risks of new local enterprises. These needs have then to be matched against accessible local resources and from this emerges a broad outline of what is feasible. It then remains for local activists to determine how to start and to develop the form of organisation most appropriate in the circumstances. It is not surprising, therefore, that in the widely differing situations of needs and resources, very different variations on the same theme are developing.

No bureaucratic organisation has developed within the trusts, and contacts between the various initiatives is maintained only through an informal network. In most instances these trusts are in an embryonic state and it remains to be seen how many will actually thrive and grow into effective groups.

What can be said about the minimum requirements to provide a fair chance for success? Given that basic needs and resources have been correctly identified and sensibly matched, it appears to be essential to have at least a core of about three highly motivated and committed local individuals who are prepared to give a great deal of their time and energy on a voluntary basis. Even so, unless they have sufficient backing from significant local organisations and a group of voluntary workers to call upon, it will be very difficult for them to achieve much. In addition, it will rapidly become essential to be able to appoint a highly qualified and motivated person to act as full-time executive officer of the Trust. This necessarily means the provision of something like £20,000 p.a. in salaries, expenses and overheads for a period of about three years by which time the organisation should be largely self-supporting. Another vital requirement is that it should be the kind of operation with which local entrepreneurs will feel comfortable and will happily associate. It is not sufficient to have a product that the customer needs: they must also be attracted to the organisation that offers it. Probably most people who could make good use of a Local Enterprise

Trust will be most attracted to an organisation which itself is clearly seen to be enterprising. Perhaps therefore, a Trust that is itself engaged in commercial ventures may have more credibility to its clients than would otherwise be the case.

What can be expected of a Local Enterprise Trust in more concrete terms? Given that its aim is to stimulate and assist new local growth and also to reduce risk and prevent unnecessary failure during the first few vulnerable years of infancy, the range of potential services that it may provide is extensive. The following are some examples:

— Provision of appropriately sized, low-cost work space or premises; assistance with purchasing or rental arrangements; liaison with local authorities or private sources for accommodation to be shared by a number of small firms e.g. converted warehouses and factories.

— Routine office administration services on a shared basis since in many parts of the country there is a lack of a low-cost service to handle such matters as book-keeping, PAYE, VAT etc. suitable for a small business. A LET could provide this or could assist in the choice of suitable auditors and accountants.

— Co-operative purchasing facilities; advice with terms of purchase, stock requirements etc.

— Marketing advice and assistance with choices of outlets and marketing methods; co-ordination between small businesses able to supply each other.

— Financial and legal advice including licensing, health and safety standards, franchises, import and export requirements.

— Assistance with project assessment, sources of credit, project presentation for obtaining financing.

— Shared transport and delivery arrangements.

— Debt collection.

The working end of an Local Enterprise Trust might well aim to initially create three new local businesses; one manufacturing, one retail and one service. These could provide the Trust with three things: experience in the setting up and operation of embryo small enterprises of different types, credibility as a source of advice and assistance to other new starters and finally, a source of income for the Trust.

Local Enterprise Trusts in the Making

Over the last year or two a number of groups and individuals in various parts of the country have been started with the idea of forming Local Enterprise Trusts or similar organisations. There are now more than 30 such groups and some of these are now coming into action.

West Somerset: Several people with small businesses in this area came together and formed a Small Industries Group to provide assistance to small firms and to stimulate new enterprise. Eventually a

46

full-time Development Officer was appointed and, despite very limited access to financial resources, the group is making good progress and has considerable local goodwill.

Antur Aaelhaearn: Llanaelhaearn is a rural community of some 300 people in the Llen peninsular of North Wales. Lead by the local doctor they made a determined start some seven years ago to reverse the decline of their community and in 1974 the Community Association espoused the concept of self-help and created the first community co-operative in Britain. Having built their own work centre they set about creating some new business enterprises. The work centre now houses 18 full-time employees and there are another 20 employed part-time in their own homes. Their development plan for the next three years includes the creation of a Rural Industries Centre to serve the surrounding area, and plan other similar ventures further afield.

Hackney, London: Following a year of preparation by the local authority and a few prominent members of the local business community, a Steering Committee was set up under the Chairmanship of the Director of one of these local firms. Plans are being made to establish a Hackney Business Promotion Centre to foster new enterprise in the Borough.

Although independent of the local authority, the Centre has its strong support. Funding has been obtained as part of Government aid to inner city areas and this will enable the first executive officer to be appointed.

A number of similar groups have followed from initiatives taken by major companies:—

Saint Helen's, Merseyside: Following two years of preparation the Board of Pilkington Brothers Ltd. decided to take the lead in setting up a Saint Helen's Trust as a stimulant to the development of the local economy. The firm appointed a senior executive to work full-time on the company's contribution to small enterprise creation in the area. The Trust itself will be a broadly based community organisation and co-sponsors are now being sought.

Glasgow: The commitment of the British Steel Corporation to assist in the provision of alternative employment for its redundant staff was expressed in the creation in 1974 of BSC (Industries) Ltd. — a subsidiary specifically assigned this task. Following the closure of the Clyde Iron Works, the company allocated some of the buildings to be converted into multi-occupation workshops with the intention of using these as a springboard for establishing a Local Enterprise Trust.

Runcorn: In 1976 the management of ICI (Mond Division) seconded one of its executives to work full-time co-ordinating assistance provided by the Division to local businesses with difficulties and to people who were trying to start up new enterprise. After this experience the company is now attempting to join forces with other firms and organisations in Runcorn and the surrounding area to create a Local Enterprise Trust.

These and many other similar ventures at various stages of planning and development (including Covent Garden Enterprise, Clerkenwell Workshops, Enterprise North, the Isle of Dogs Human Development Project and many others) may have quite different structures and emphases but all are aimed in some way to help the development of small business in their locations and to revive a spirit of self-help, independence and enterprise in the community.

The Interdependence of Established and New Firms
It is in the interests of major established firms to promote growth in the small business sector. There are three main reasons why this is so:—
i)   *A prosperous domestic economy* The failure of any part of the wealth creating sector of our economy is damaging to all. To many major firms it is doubly harmful. Not only do those remaining businesses have to provide some of the lost tax revenues and the added finance required for the resulting enlarged public sector or longer dole queue but many suppliers of materials and components also lose an important piece of their domestic market outlet. A prosperous domestic economy is essential for the well-being of nearly all major firms. A healthy independent sector — regularly strengthened and refreshed by the germination of new enterprises — is a vital ingredient of an industrial economy.
ii)   *A chance to concentrate* A feature of many of the most successful big companies throughout the world is the intensity of their concentration on what they perceive to be their essential business interests and expertise. They have succeeded in avoiding a proliferation of peripheral activities through a conscious and controlled policy of subcontracting. A pre-requisite for their success is a network of small firms and a responsiveness within the local economy so that new enterprise can rapidly form to meet changing requirements. Where this is not available, a major company may be forced to be self-reliant for more than it wishes and this may detract from its primary concern.
iii)   *Freedom to change* Whilst there are many factors that limit the ability of big firms to adapt to changing circumstances, one in particular appears to be worsening. The achievement of efficient levels of manning is a necessary condition for successful business. More often than not the replacement of old methods by new ones requires a degree of de-manning involving redundancies. Where there is a hungry labour market locally, the difficulties can usually be surmounted, but where alternative local employment opportunities are few, a company may find immovable obstacles to change.

Major established firms have a lot to offer particularly if advice and assistance to small firms can be channelled through Local Enterprise Trust-type organisations. Such firms can help with many of the functions of the Trusts discussed earlier. In particular they may be able to:

- assist small firms by providing business or financial credibility through a direct trading relationship or by their general association with a Local Enterprise Trust;
- provide help with expertise and training;
- release spare land or buildings;
- make available ideas that the large firm has not itself developed or commercialised because they were not considered to be of sufficient big company interest;
- establish a new small business advice centre;
- pass on a going concern because the major firm wishes to disinvest a part of its existing business but wishes it to be continued independently;
- assist its manpower surplus in establishing a new business;
- assist with surplus materials and equipment;
- provide financial aid to small firms, e.g. chemical manufacturers assisting plastics processing firms;
- identify market opportunities for local small firms to replace imports;
- help small firms with technical development work that big firms themselves might also benefit from;
- avoid embarrassing their small suppliers by paying promptly!

Clearly there could be many interdependencies between new and established firms. Above and beyond all that, however, is the increasing realisation that big companies have a citizenship responsibility and must play their part in overcoming national and local difficulties. It is becoming more widely accepted that, for example, worsening structural unemployment amongst young manual workers and school leavers will not be solved by big, capital intensive business investment. Sustained growth in the small firm sector offers much more hope and many major established firms are now beginning to appreciate that small businesses urgently need their help.

Summary of necessary conditions for a successful Local Enterprise Trust
Given the experiences of the Local Enterprise Trust-type initiatives taken to date, it would appear that any individual or group contemplating such a venture should give consideration to the following list of requirements:
- A small core group of committed individuals in the community who are prepared to work voluntarily for up to several years to help set up the Trust.
- Adequate and firm backing from significant local organisations e.g. local government, business, community bodies, labour movements etc.
- A highly competent and socially motivated entrepreneur to act as chief executive of the Trust on a salaried full-time basis.

— A sufficient group of volunteers to provide professional help and advice to the Trust and to small business ventures.
— A planned programme of income-generating activities that will enable the Local Enterprise Trust to become self-supporting within about three years.
— A supply of 'pump priming' finance (mainly from local sources) to meet the needs of the Trust during the first few years.
— A clearly defined set of functions to fulfil and a corresponding programme of tasks to perform based on a careful analysis of local needs, resources and opportunities.
— Early practical demonstrations of the effectiveness of the Local Enterprise Trust in order to develop credibility in the community and generate goodwill and an enterprising spirit.

6

Education for a New World

Until the second half of this century the rate of social change was sufficiently slow to safely assume that the world into which children would grow would be much the same as that into which they were born. That can no longer be assumed. The present situation is different in two important respects:—
— the rate of change is now very rapid indeed;
— we are at an important turning point in our national development and in the development of the rest of the world.
It is consequently quite hopeless to attempt to describe in clear and definitive ways the kind of world into which new generations will grow. This does not mean, however, that there is nothing worth saying that is positive and relevant to their upbringing and education.

It is quite certain that the future will not be very much like the recent past, therefore our children need to be prepared from an early age to be adaptable. Since uncertainty will be an ever-present factor for at least the next few generations it is more important than ever to foster social values that transcend the particular transformations the future will bring. In a climate of such uncertainty nothing could be more destructive individually or socially than the feeling that there is no firm foundation for anything at all. No matter what precise path of development emerges, the continuation of civilised basic human values is essential and education both formal and informal has a vital role to play.

It is fairly certain that, in an age of easy mass communication, there will be great clashes of competing ideas, ideologies and cultures just at the time when the need is primarily to reduce social and international tensions. A key role of education must be to teach children the tricks of propaganda — no matter where it comes from — and to help them develop keen and critical minds. Children must be brought up to understand something that our present system of distant authority and unnecessary complexity makes very elusive i.e. that the future can be shaped, for better or worse, by the actions of present generations. The influence of the new generation of young people is profoundly important and they will need to develop a strong sense of personal responsibility towards shaping the future. This will be a hopeless task for education to fulfil alone without accompanying changes in society at large. The indifference presently displayed by large sections of the young is a direct consequence of the uncaring attitude shown by society towards the material and natural world, of the failure of society to create conditions for challenging and meaningful employment and of the mass production system which through the promotion of advertising-led consumer dreamland fantasies has created an unbridgeable and destructive gap between expectations and reality.

In what will certainly be a crowded and hungry world we must find ways to diminish the material expectations of young people in the developed countries and to replace those expectations with other more socially converging and environmentally sound ambitions. A contribution towards this which would also lessen the tensions within and between countries could come from a greater appreciation of our material heritage and man's relationship with it. We must learn to build our own material economy largely within the scope of our national resources. Obviously, education can help create a sense of responsibility for the natural world and an attitude of stewardship towards it. The need to carefully husband and conserve resources which are non-renewable and in short supply will require a rebirth in the sense of value of material things which has been lost with the industrial age and the coming of the throw-away society.

As the limits to material growth are experienced it is likely that a much broader sense of social justice will need to grow out of the very limited financial interpretation that has prevailed so far. Not only may the privileged white-collar worker be required through economic necessity to exercise increasing skills in do-it-yourself activities, he or she may also be required to spend some of their life undertaking some of the less pleasant tasks that society requires to be performed. However, even with the greatly reduced availability of energy and power which our children may experience it is still most probable that there need be no return to back-breaking toil. Indeed, there will very likely be a continuing decline in unskilled labouring employment and an increasing need for a highly skilled population, not only to provide for the needs of industry, commerce and services, but also to equip individuals for a far more do-it-yourself lifestyle. However, the distaste for manual work will have to be changed partly through education where the development of balanced training of hand and brain will be of the highest importance.

Our new education programme should aim to help children at school to understand some important things about the technological society in which they are growing up and, in particular, about its strengths and weaknesses. They must realise that important changes are taking place in the world which will effect them both as consumers and at work. Technologies are at the centre of these changes. Perhaps the most important aspect of the required new educational approach concerns the changes in attitudes and values that will be involved in living in the 'quality of life' age and in developing and utilising technologies appropriate to it. This means that education must be approached on a very broad front rather than from a narrow conventionally scientific point of view. For example, it will be important for children to understand that all ages prior to the industrial era were times in which there was little economic growth and that a future 'no-growth' period will, in an historical sense, be a return to normality. Although education for the new world must be concerned with very practical areas of knowledge, a great opportunity will have been lost if these broader issues are not provided as a unifying context.

Ideas for topics with considerable educational value which would be of interest in planning a balanced course around the appropriate technology theme include:

i) The extent of our dependence as a nation upon
   — our own natural resources, and
   — imported food, raw materials and fuel; how this has changed throughout history and how it will need to change in the future.

ii) The differences between
   — ecologically well-balanced rural community life, and
   — the present ecologically unsatisfactory industrialised society and the damage that is being done to the natural environment.

iii) The fundamental importance to all human societies of reliable supplies of wholesome food, clean water and air and our dependence on the most important resource of all — the soil. The principles of organic farming as opposed to present industrial methods.

iv) The values and priorities of societies which were not pre-occupied with economic growth and how these were influenced by religious and philosophies prevailing at the time.

v) The effect of the mass production system on the diminishing availability of regionally varied goods, architecture, dishes etc.

vi) The effect of the mass production system on the life-costs of products; planned obsolescence; the role of the advertising industry.

vii) The benefits that have been derived from modern technology in reducing poverty and disease, increasing opportunities for recreational and cultural activities and in reducing physical toil.

The theme of appropriate technology provides opportunities for learning by doing. As a result of an initiative by the Community Service Volunteers, a "Kit on Appropriate Technology for Schools and Community Groups" has been produced under the guidance of Ann Griffiths*. In addition to sections on Windpower, Methane, Solar

*Available from CSV, 237 Pentonville Road, London N1 9NJ or from ITDG, 9 King Street, London WC2E 8HN.

Energy, Recycling, Transport, Printing, Farming, Dyeing and Spinning and Weaving, there is a valuable description of the one term "Possible Futures" General Studies course at Pocklington School in Yorkshire run by the heads of biology, English, design and the School Chaplain. Such an interdisciplinary approach at school level is likely to be an extremely useful vehicle for developing thinking in appropriate technology.

In higher education, many would argue that we now have too many universities and that the decline in Technical Colleges and Colleges of Arts and Crafts, which offered alternative outlets from the conventional, purely academic educational stream, has been a big loss. Nowadays, no longer do students learn design and art and crafts technology — they learn to write about it instead! It is quite astonishing that the total annual number of people qualifying in production engineering in Britain has fallen from 1134 in 1967 to 294 in 1975 — and this in a period of great expansion in higher education. The trend is disastrous for the future of manufacturing and will effect big, medium and small firms alike. Prior to the expansion of universities and polytechnics many able school leavers entered industry and acquired professional qualifications by evening study and day release. This vital supply of production engineers has been cut off almost at a stroke as these young people enter colleges and opt for almost anything but production engineering. Some of the responsibility for the low esteem in which this side of engineering is held rests with the schools where there is a big bias towards traditional scholarship as opposed to creative and multi-disciplinary arts and sciences. But the higher education system must play its part in encouraging bright young minds into the field by redesigning courses to be more creative and problem-solving and more clearly relevant to wider social issues and concerns.

Fortunately there are signs of change. The Open University Faculty of Technology offers courses in design which are likely to stimulate and attract many different kinds of people into the field. In Swindon a 'University of the Community' is being started that aims to produce graduates of high ability who develop their talents as members of interdisciplinary work groups operating within a socially comprehensive environment, learning through involvement in the study of really significant problems.

The informal sector cannot do a great deal to make up for the shortcomings of the formal education and training systems but they can and are doing something useful. One example concerns Training Workshops which hope to provide training for some of those people who cannot find a way into the formal system.

The problem of providing training for would-be entrepreneurs who are planning to set up small businesses is one for which no satisfactory solution exists in this country. It is often felt that the conventional classroom situation seldom meets the needs of this rather unusual group of people. An interesting experiment is being started by the Urban and Economic Development Group in Covent Garden. Encouraged by some of the Local Enterprise Trust network and mindful of comparable schemes in Scandinavia, plans have been prepared for a trial training programme. This will consist of about six weekend workshops for a carefully selected group who will be given time to develop the plans for their businesses in an environment where they can tap the expertise of some experienced small business people and interact with each other on common problems.

But that these encouraging changes are not yet occurring on a sufficient scale — particularly in formal education — was recently brought home strongly to me personally. A young man, recently graduated with a good arts degree, was seeking guidance on what he should do with his life. In the course of conversation it became clear that under no circumstances would he spend any more time — even part-time — in one of our educational institutions; not even if it was only to learn a craft. I have come across plenty of people who have been alienated by their experience of school, but never before had I heard such condemnation of the whole system — including higher education — by one of its recent successful products. He was clearly very angry that after more than fifteen years he was little better prepared to stand on his own feet and launch out into the world than he was when he started school. Despite his academic honours he felt that the educational system had totally failed him and his contemporaries and that all he had been prepared for was to become a dependent individual occupying a cosy and safe position in some big institution. This he refuses to do and I admire him for his courage in rejecting the easy option. He will need all the courage he can muster because, at the age of 22 and with no marketable skill or know-how, he faces a very difficult five or ten years; though I believe that his education may prove a little more useful than he expects. When I reflect on the very small number of independent people operating in our society that I meet who are graduates, I cannot help but feel a good deal of sympathy for my young friend's anger.

Far from leading progressive social change, for the most part our education system is some way behind and has failed to adapt to the changing world. The new generation has been badly let down and this must not be allowed to happen to future generations.

7

Technologies: The Right to Choose

Despite the enormous influence of technology on the lives of everyone, very little public discussion of the options available takes place in this country. When it does, it tends to be concerned with dramatic examples like Concorde or the Channel Tunnel or with sources of potential danger such as nuclear power stations or plants processing dangerous chemicals. Important as these topics are, they are no more than the tip of a technology iceberg since many other issues, which in many respects have more immediate and far reaching consequences for large numbers of people, are seldom given an airing.

Choices of technology have been made and continue to be made with little or no involvement from those concerned with and affected by the outcomes of those choices. It has been tacitly assumed that technology choice is a subject for professional expert judgement. Decisions have been the exclusive perogative of a very small group of industrialists, bureaucrats and professionals and these decisions have been constrained by little more than the crude economics of a balance sheet.

At any time it is important that basic choices which can influence the direction in which society will develop are open to informed public discussion, after which it is the people's right to choose that must be honoured above all sectional interests. At the present turning point in the evolution of our society it is vitally important that this democratic right to choose be exercised: the choice must be real. The growth of technology assessment as seen in some countries is unsatisfactory since it is invariably the "powers that be" who act as witness, judge and jury in their own case, when technology implications are assessed by the same agencies that promote them. Neither are special interest groups the answer. Whilst many of these (for example, the Conservation Society, the Council for the Protection of Rural England etc.) do valiant work in opposing changes which, from their point of view, are undesirable, the ensuing struggle is one of confrontation between conflicting interest groups each claiming to be acting in the public's interest. In truth the public is not represented at all and the real consensus wishes are unknown.

Whilst it would be naive to pretend that a convenient consensus can be obtained or that local and national interests will always coincide, there is clearly an urgent need for wider public information and debate. Helplessness in the face of bureaucratic and expert decision-making is another important factor in the current widespread social malaise. At least four areas require action to facilitate the right to choose:

— The general public must be alerted to the fact that we are at a watershed in the course of our technological development and that important decisions in the choice of technology have to be taken.
— The public must be informed of the options that are available, and the probable favourable and unfavourable consequences of each must be fully and openly explored and exposed.
— An opportunity for open public debate must be provided before decisions are made and options closed.
— New independent institutional arrangements need to be created in order to articulate the public will on key issues, and to ensure that the voice of minority groups is heard. This should result in the development of recommendations concerning technology choices.

Such recommendations must be directed at Parliament so that where appropriate they can be translated into legislation and proper influence exerted on decision-making agencies.

One way in which such a process could be initiated is through the creation of an early warning group charged with the tasks of:—

— monitoring all significant areas of future technological change;
— selecting those examples that, because of important potential consequences on society, require informed and focussed public debate;
— organising a means of alerting the public to the need for information and debate;
— setting up the mechanism for such debate and where necessary creating ad hoc organisations appropriately.

In order to ensure the independence of the recommendations on technology choice eventually acted upon at Parliamentary level, a separate body should be set up to undertake the analysis and synthesis of public debate and to arrange for the publication of such recommendations.

Conclusion
There is much room for innovation in the precise form of institutions established to inform on and interpret the necessary debate on the future of our technology. But it is vital that this debate occur and that

it is not left to the experts to make the key decisions. Whilst their input is essential, the far-reaching social, economic and environmental consequences involved are the concern of us all.

Before any decisions are made, however, we must realise that what we are considering is a change in the direction of technology development. This is needed to negotiate a difficult period of transition from indiscriminate and unrestrained economic growth, which has benefited a few at great social cost, towards a kind of development which will benefit society as a whole and which will give due regard to our environment. Ultimately, our technologies exist to promote human and social ends and not purely economic ones. Their overriding objectives should be to encourage social harmony and economic equality, thereby contributing to a lessening of both internal and international tension.

FORTHCOMING PUBLICATIONS FROM INTERMEDIATE TECHNOLOGY PUBLICATIONS LTD.

The Power Guide: A Catalogue of Small-Scale Power Equipment by Peter Fraenkel. A comprehensive catalogue of equipment from more than 300 manufacturers from all over the world. It includes diesel, petrol, steam and gas engines; solar and battery power; water-powered and wind-driven engines; turbines; hydro ram pumps; generators; plus control equipment and sources of further information. Fully illustrated and indexed. Due in February 1979.

Accounting & Book-keeping for the Small Building Contractor and *Financial Planning for the Small Building Contractor* by Derek Miles. The first two series of three volumes designed as self-teaching material for students and entrepreneurs in the building industry. Practical exercises and simple accounting forms are included. The subjects covered include: organising the office; basic book-keeping; analysis sheets; profit and loss; planning the year's work; job programmes; cash flow; investment decisions; billing procedures; work study techniques; estimating and tendering. Illustrated. Vol.1 due in November 1978; Vol.2 in December 1978.

Towards Village Industry by Berg, Nimpuno and van Zwanenberg. This book is primarily concerned with village industry and cottage industries in the very poorest countries, in the context of community development. The basic premise of the book is that industrialisation of the rural areas in developing countries must play a vital role, and that mechanisation of agricultural methods and production will have to develop parallel to this. Fully illustrated. Due in December 1978.

The Work of a Co-operative Committee by Peter Yeo and the Co-operatives Panel, Intermediate Technology Development Group. This booklet explains in detail the role of the committee in the operations of a co-operative. It is written as a programmed learning text for the staff of co-operatives, for use in group training or individual study. Due in November 1978.

Orders from US and Canada should be sent to our North American agents, International Scholarly Book Services Inc., P.O. Box 555, Forest Grove, Oregon 97116, USA.

All other orders should be sent to Intermediate Technology Publications Ltd, 9 King Street, London WC2E 8HN, UK.

SOCIAL SCIENCE LIBRARY

Manor Road Building
Manor Road
Oxford OX1 3UQ
Tel: (2)71093 (enquiries and renewals)
http://www.ssl.ox.ac.uk

This is a NORMAL LOAN item.

We will email you a reminder before this item is due.

Please see http://www.ssl.ox.ac.uk/lending.html
for details on:

- loan policies; these are also displayed on the notice boards and in our library guide.

- how to check when your books are due back.

- how to renew your books, including information on the maximum number of renewals. Items may be renewed if not reserved by another reader. Items must be renewed before the library closes on the due date.

- level of fines; fines are charged on overdue books.

Please note that this item may be recalled during Term.

RECRUITMENT AND SELECTION

P R Plumbley

Plumbley/Endicott & Associates Ltd

Institute of Personnel Management

First published 1968
Reprinted twice 1969
Second edition 1974
Third edition 1976
Reprinted 1978, 1981
Fourth edition 1985

© Institute of Personnel Management 1968, 1974, 1976 and 1985

British Library Cataloguing in Publication Data
Plumbley, Philip
  Recruitment and selection.—4th ed.
  1. Recruiting of employees
  I. Title   II. Institute of Personnel Management
  658.3'11   HF5549.5.R44

ISBN 0 85292 342 2

Typeset by Cotswold Typesetting Ltd, Gloucester
Printed in Great Britain by Dotesios Printers Ltd